Traces of What Was

THE AZRIELI SERIES OF HOLOCAUST SURVIVOR MEMOIRS:
PREVIOUSLY PUBLISHED TITLES

Traces of What Was
Steve Rotschild-Galerkin

THE AZRIELI FOUNDATION
www.azrielifoundation.org

Cover and book design by Mark Goldstein
Endpaper maps by Martin Gilbert
Map on page xxiii by François Blanc
How Many Bob Dylans? on page 51 courtesy of David Suissa, adapted and reprinted from *Olam*, Summer 2002.

LIBRARY AND ARCHIVES CANADA CATALOGUING IN PUBLICATION

Rotschild-Galerkin, S. Z., 1933-, author
    Traces of what was / Steve Rotschild-Galerkin.

(The Azrieli series of Holocaust survivor memories ; 6)
Includes bibliographical references and index.
ISBN 978-1-897470-44-2 (pbk.)

1. Rotschild-Galerkin, S. Z. 2. Holocaust, Jewish (1939–1945) – Lithuania – Vilnius – Personal narratives. 3. World War, 1939–1945 – Personal narratives, Jewish. 4. Jews – Lithuania – Vilnius – Biography. I. Title. II. Series: Azrieli series of Holocaust survivor memoirs. Series ; VI

DS135.L53R66 2014   940.53'18092   C2014-906096-3

PRINTED IN CANADA

The Azrieli Series of Holocaust Survivor Memoirs

Naomi Azrieli, Publisher

Jody Spiegel, Program Director
Arielle Berger, Managing Editor
Elizabeth Lasserre, Senior Editor, French-Language Editions
Aurélien Bonin, French-Language Educational Outreach and Events
Catherine Person, Quebec Educational Outreach and Events
Elin Beaumont, English-Language Educational Outreach and Events
Tim MacKay, New Media and Marketing

Susan Roitman, Executive Assistant and Office Manager (Toronto)
Mary Mellas, Executive Assistant and Human Resources (Montreal)
Eric Bélisle, Administrative Assistant

Mark Goldstein, Art Director
François Blanc, Cartographer
Bruno Paradis, Layout, French-Language Editions

Contents

Series Preface:
In their own words. . .

In telling these stories, the writers have liberated themselves. For so many years we did not speak about it, even when we became free people living in a free society. Now, when at last we are writing about what happened to us in this dark period of history, knowing that our stories will be read and live on, it is possible for us to feel truly free. These unique historical documents put a face on what was lost, and allow readers to grasp the enormity of what happened to six million Jews – one story at a time.

David J. Azrieli, C.M., C.Q., M.Arch
Holocaust survivor and founder, The Azrieli Foundation

Since the end of World War II, over 30,000 Jewish Holocaust survivors have immigrated to Canada. Who they are, where they came from, what they experienced and how they built new lives for themselves and their families are important parts of our Canadian heritage. The Azrieli Foundation's Holocaust Survivor Memoirs Program was established to preserve and share the memoirs written by those who survived the twentieth-century Nazi genocide of the Jews of Europe and later made their way to Canada. The program is guided by the conviction that each survivor of the Holocaust has a remarkable story to tell, and that such stories play an important role in education about tolerance and diversity.

Millions of individual stories are lost to us forever. By preserving the stories written by survivors and making them widely available to a broad audience, the Azrieli Foundation's Holocaust Survivor Memoirs Program seeks to sustain the memory of all those who perished at the hands of hatred, abetted by indifference and apathy. The personal accounts of those who survived against all odds are as different as the people who wrote them, but all demonstrate the courage, strength, wit and luck that it took to prevail and survive in such terrible adversity. The memoirs are also moving tributes to people – strangers and friends – who risked their lives to help others, and who, through acts of kindness and decency in the darkest of moments, frequently helped the persecuted maintain faith in humanity and courage to endure. These accounts offer inspiration to all, as does the survivors' desire to share their experiences so that new generations can learn from them.

The Holocaust Survivor Memoirs Program collects, archives and publishes these distinctive records and the print editions are available free of charge to libraries, educational institutions and Holocaust-education programs across Canada. They are also available for sale to the general public at bookstores. All revenues to the Azrieli Foundation from the sales of the Azrieli Series of Holocaust Survivor Memoirs go toward the publishing and educational work of the memoirs program.

The Azrieli Foundation would like to express appreciation to the following people for their invaluable efforts in producing this book: Sherry Dodson (Maracle Press), Sir Martin Gilbert, Farla Klaiman, Andrea Knight, Malcolm Lester, Therese Parent, David Suissa, and Margie Wolfe and Emma Rodgers of Second Story Press.

About the Glossary

The following memoir contains a number of terms, concepts and historical references that may be unfamiliar to the reader. For information on major organizations; significant historical events and people; geographical locations; religious and cultural terms; and foreign-language words and expressions that will help give context and background to the events described in the text, please see the glossary beginning on page 89.

Introduction

How we approach, read and appreciate Holocaust survivor memoirs is not how we approach, read and appreciate most books, and rightly so. We may read a Holocaust memoir and be struck by its aesthetics, style and dramatic story, but we also value the simple fact that it exists, is real and true and accessible, that its contents are known and knowable. Holocaust memoirs are in many ways memorials in book form, offering a way to access, cherish and safeguard memories that are critical to access, cherish and safeguard. Collectively, survivor memoirs represent the ongoing attempt to build, restore and maintain not what was lost – for that is a tragically impossible goal – but the *memory* of what was lost. In this sense, the reader is not only a reader, but also a *receiver*. The scholar David Patterson has written that the reader of a Holocaust memoir "must become not an interpreter of texts but a mender of the world, a part of the recovery that this memory demands."[1]

From a literary perspective, the Holocaust memoir is *kadosh*, holy – it has something of the sacred, of the *sui generis*, of the incommensurable. To discuss a Holocaust memoir purely in terms of style is to

---

1   David Patterson, *Sun Turned to Darkness* (New York: Syracuse University Press, 1998), 12.

miss the point entirely. And yet, memoirs are not necessarily only about being true and accessible; the great and lasting memoirs are, without exception, literary works of the highest calibre. Primo Levi, Elie Wiesel and Anne Frank did not merely tell their extraordinary stories, they told their stories extraordinarily well. Their writing style – their formal innovation, exacting prose – are qualities integral to the experience of reading and absorbing their stories, of having the kind of experience the author intended.

In this manner, Steve Rotschild's memoir is a rare and special book, a memoir – the story of a Jewish boy in a war zone, in a ghetto, in hiding – written with the utmost skill, care and love. A professor of mine once described literature as that which cannot be summarized; literature is what's beyond or beneath the hard facts – it is the difference between knowing an author's story and feeling a person's experience. It's why stories aren't told in bullet points.

That said, even in bullet points Mr. Rotschild's story is gripping and terrifying: hiding in the Vilna ghetto; living under a false identity with a Russian family; his father's death; escaping the ghetto with his mother; hiding, again, at HKP, a forced labour camp; hiding, again, behind a fake wall while German soldiers searched for the children. But this memoir is so much more than an assemblage of harrowing events. It is patient, subtle, deeply felt, finely wrought and considered. It is, at times, wonderfully strange. There are moments of delight, moments of wonder; it is continually vibrant and alive.

Although *Traces of What Was* contains terror and tragedy, it would be a mistake to say it is *about* the terror and tragedy. Rotschild's uncle's wedding –which took place in 1938, before the war, before the Germans occupied Vilna – is recounted with as much care and attention as his experience in the ghetto. His stay at his grandparents' house, where he learned to play with the country children, is as formative and significant as his pretending to be the Christian nephew of a Russian family. The overall effect is unaffected, genuine. Rotschild is not only offering his experience as a witness to history, as the testimony of a survivor often does, he is, in the manner of the artist, offering himself. It is a special book wherein every sentence feels both necessary and surprising.

As a reader, I'm amazed by Mr. Rotschild's recall of people, events and places, how he commands memories of colours, sounds, faces, clothes. As a writer, I'm humbled by how effectively he deploys these details, how deftly he creates momentum, urgency, setting, realness and familiarity. There are countless examples. His "grandparents' house was built of square logs that turned a dark mahogany colour with age." In a remarkable passage, Rotschild describes his fear of the nights in the ghetto – not the dark but the *sounds:* the "chorus of snoring in the stillness of the night… the distinctive… ping of a strong stream of urine hitting the metal of the copper pot, and the sound one older man made by grinding his teeth." These are sentences one wants to hear read aloud. Rotschild returns, again and again, to sounds: screams in the ghetto hospital; steel-shod boots on the other side of a false wall.

Throughout, Steve Rotschild is bravely, astonishingly unsentimental. The details, no matter how horrifying, are recounted matter-of-factly but never coldly. About his father's death, Rotschild writes: "I suspect my father lacked what I think of as the traits of a survivor… I was nine years old and had never really gotten to know my father. What I know of him is mostly secondhand from people who knew him and whom I met after the war. I know what he looked like from a photograph, on the back of which is a sample of his beautiful handwriting." That's all.

"Unsentimental" does not mean unemotional or distant. It means naked, unadorned, raw. Rotschild's account is never less than piercingly honest and courageous, and, for that reason, it's occasionally brutal – there is no wistfulness, no sentimental or semantic cushion. "That's what I saw; that's what I remember," Rotschild writes.

Books like Rotschild's remind us that the worth of a memoir is not only measured by what it does or does not add to our knowledge, but, moreover, what it allows us to access, to tap into, to empathize with. If history is the study of the masses, of political and military currents, of dates and events and locations, of *data*, then memoir is about a boy and the people he loves, the people he loses, about the basements and attics his family must hide in, about fear and longing, hunger and hope, about the terrifying sound of snoring in an overcrowded room in the ghetto, about instinct, endurance, playfulness and spirit. Books like this remind us that the Holocaust isn't a subject that can be represented by a section in the library or two shelves in your living room. History *happened*, and it happened to people; look closely enough and the smooth facade of History is revealed to be woven from millions of strands of histories – personal, intimate stories, of deaths of unfamous fathers, of games of hide-and-go-seek, of names otherwise forgotten, of names not famous enough for the history books. Stories like Steve Rotschild's. History might be defined broadly as the scientific study and analysis of relevant documents towards a coherent narrative. What stories do, though, is let us into that narrative – they allow an empathetic grip on unimaginable events and impossible numbers. Reading a well-wrought story of what happened to one affects profoundly how we read the history of the many.

Steve Rotschild's story is a story played out on the grandest historical stage, a story knitted onto history. In 1939, Rotschild, then six years old, was one of the approximately 60,000 Jews comprising more than 40 per cent of Vilna's population. In August of that year, Germany and the Soviet Union signed a secret treaty, known as the Molotov-Ribbentrop Pact, that carved up most of Eastern Europe into Nazi and Soviet "spheres of influence." In September 1939, the Red Army occupied Vilna, in then-Poland. Rotschild experienced his first antisemitic incident; there was a run on his mother's grocery's store; his father was fired from his accounting job at a radio factory; and his parents opened an ice cream parlour. On June 22, 1941, Germany reneged on the treaty and invaded Lithuania, and within a couple of weeks occupied Vilna, which had become part of

Lithuania in October 1939. At this time, Rotschild was at his grandparents' home in Popishok, a small village outside Vilna, watching his
grandfather *daven* and his grandmother prepare *cholent* and gefilte
fish. In the following weeks, German authorities issued a series of
increasingly severe edicts against Jews, prohibiting radios and use of
sidewalks, instituting curfews, mandating the wearing of visible yellow stars. Jews began to be taken from the streets, and soon from
their homes. Most of those rounded up were eventually taken to
Ponary, a forest about eleven kilometres outside the city, where they
were shot and buried in enormous open-air pits originally designed
to hold fuel tankers.

On September 6, 1941, German and municipal authorities ordered
all Vilna Jews into two ghettos. At the outset the ghettos contained
about 20,000 Jews – at least 45,000 had already been murdered.
Through a series of *aktionen*, violent roundups, the second, smaller
ghetto was liquidated in late October, around the time Rotschild's
mother smuggled him out of the ghetto. In early 1942, life in the
ghetto stabilized and Rotschild returned to the ghetto to live with his
mother. They escaped again just weeks before the remaining ghetto
was fully and finally liquidated in September 1943, walking "on the
outside" seeking shelter and eventually finding relative safety, strange
as it may seem to today's reader, in a forced labour camp managed
by a sympathetic Nazi officer, Karl Plagge. In the autumn of 1944, the
Soviets liberated Lithuania, and Rothschild and his mother began the
painful process of rebuilding their lives. Many of Rothschild's relatives did not survive; most of those who did eventually immigrated
to Israel, the United States or Canada.

What's most remarkable about Rotschild's memoir is how, by vir-
tue of its prose and form, it accesses a perspective that's nearly always
inaccessible: that of a child. One of many examples is when, toward
the end of 1941, a few months after the establishment of the Vilna
ghetto, Rotschild is living outside the ghetto, hiding his identity.
Every two or three weeks he walks into town to visit his parents, who

are working and hiding in a warehouse. On one of these trips, he is given a cookie by a German soldier, and though he fears it contains poison, he eats it anyway. Now, Mr. Rotschild could have written this anecdote like I just did: bluntly, to the point, without texture. Instead he writes, in simple, effective prose, about being transfixed by the splendour and power of a German soldier, about the solider beckoning him from across the street and giving him the cookie, about summoning the courage to do something as normally banal as taking a bite of a cookie, and then, "I took a small bite and tasted no poison." With this description, you do not merely know Rotschild's story, you experience it as he did, as an eight-year-old to whom the fear of a poisoned cookie makes perfect sense, who, despite his uncertainty, cannot help but take a bite, because it is 1941 in German-occupied Vilna and he is holding *a cookie with sprinkles*, and so he bites the cookie and when he doesn't taste poison he is relieved, safe.

It feels nearly miraculous, being able to tap into not just the experience, but the experience of a child who does not quite understand the experience, who endures one of the most traumatic events in history but is nonetheless still a child. A six-year-old sees his country invaded, Jews rounded up and walled in and murdered; he sees bodies and limbs poking out from rubble; he lives through his father's death and the disappearance of nearly his entire extended family. And yet, there are as many moments of delight and playfulness as there are of despair. In his grandparents' kitchen he is bitten by an almost-dead fish. He digs for gold in a potato field and finds a "well-preserved ham." Moments like these comprise the real, textured, weird, inimitable experiences of a child. In the HKP work camp, Rotschild and his friends played *melina*, hiding, "watching the comings and goings of trucks." Children played here, too.

Though *Traces of What Was* is about Steve Rotschild's remarkable childhood, it is also about Steve Rotschild, a man in his early seventies in Toronto, remembering Steve Rotschild's childhood. The present and past narratives are braided. Rotschild, in 2002, wanders a

Toronto cemetery, spots a coyote; clears a felled tree from the road to his cabin; asks his mother at her 90th birthday party what year it is. A significant part of the memoir is dedicated to Rotschild's meanderings and wanderings in the Canadian countryside, at the cabin, in the cemetery, noticing worms and winds and tombstones, describing raccoons, rabbits, robins. This is not supplementary material: Steve Rotschild circa 2002 is as central to the book as Steve Rotschild circa 1941. This is living memory. Sometimes, in our enthusiasm to capture a survivor's story, to record and index every minute detail of a first-hand Shoah experience, we forget that a survivor is not exhaustively described as a "survivor," but is someone who's suffered a stranger and more tragic life than we can ever know. We must look to the survivor not with intent to extract – they are not resources to mine, they are not museum exhibitions. Rather, we must sit at their feet and *know* – not only of what they went through, but also of them. Memory cannot be divorced from its bearer.

I have never met Steve Rotschild, I do not know him beyond the glimpse his book offers, but what a rich glimpse it is. I finished this book feeling like I *do* know him, like I gained some measure of understanding of a soul that went through what I do not and cannot fully understand. It's through the refraction of spirits as expansive as Rotschild's that we access and receive and transmit the memories we do not possess but nevertheless may not forget.

Menachem Kaiser
University of Michigan
2014

SUGGESTIONS FOR FURTHER READING

Arad, Yitzhak. *Ghetto in Flames: The Struggle and Destruction of the Jews in Vilna in the Holocaust.* New York: KTAV Publishing House, Inc., 1980.
Bak, Samuel. *Painted in Words.* Bloomington: Indiana University Press, 2001.

Dawidowicz, Lucy. *From That Place and Time: A Memoir, 1938–1947.* New Brunswick, NJ: Rutgers University Press, 2008.

Good, Michael. *The Search for Major Plagge: The Nazi Who Saved Jews.* New York: Fordham University Press, 2006.

Kruk, Herman. *The Last Days of the Jerusalem of Lithuania: Chronicles from the Vilna Ghetto and the Camps, 1939-1944.* Ed. Benjamin Harshav; Trans. Barbara Harshav. New Haven, CT: Yale University Press, 2002.

Patterson, David. *Sun Turned to Darkness: Memory and Recovery in the Holocaust Memoir.* New York: Syracuse University Press, 1998.

Porat, Dina. "The Holocaust in Lithuania." In *The Final Solution: Origins and Implementation.* Ed. David Cesarani. Oxford: Routledge, 1994, 159-174.

Porat, Dina. *The Fall of a Sparrow: The Life and Times of Abba Kovner.* Stanford: Stanford University Press, 2009.

Shawn, Karen, and Keren Goldfrad, eds. *The Call of Memory: Learning About the Holocaust Through Memory.* New Jersey: Ben Yehuda Press, 2008.

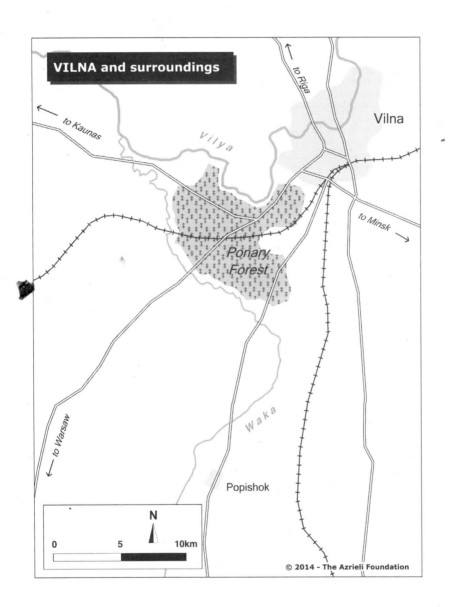

VILNA and surroundings

to Riga

Vilna

to Kaunas

Vilya

Ponary
Forest

to Minsk

to Warsaw

Waka

Popishok

N

0   5   10km

© 2014 - The Azrieli Foundation

To leave a trace for future generations of those who came before them, of what happened in the great annihilation of 1941–1945, and a snapshot of life at that time, in lieu of the photographs that perished with the people in the conflagration.

To my mother, a strong and very brave woman loved by everyone.

Popishok

It is early morning in December. The sun is just rising over the tall condominium buildings about a kilometre away, reflecting strongly off the polished surfaces of the marble headstones in the large cemetery. This is where I walk to stay healthy and alive.

It is very cold, and as I turn my back to the sun, the west wind stings the area of my face not covered by my toque. Most of the names and inscriptions on the graves along the twisting paths are familiar to me because I walk here several times each week, as I have for the past seven years. I walk an average of twenty-four kilometres a week and have covered a distance of close to 14,000 kilometres since I was diagnosed with heart disease. I'm hoping to avoid open-heart surgery, which I dread. I have, however, no dread of the dead, and prefer the quiet of the cemetery to the noise of city streets.

My walk lasts a little over an hour and with nothing to occupy my mind, I recall the first walk I can remember. It was in the fall of 1938, just before my fifth birthday, when my paternal grandmother took me to see my first movie, *Snow White and the Seven Dwarfs*.

～

We lived in the back of my mother's little grocery store on the outskirts of Vilna and, although I don't remember how we got to the movie theatre in town, I have a vivid recollection of returning home from the city. I remember holding on to my grandmother's hand, a woman of rather small stature, but very dignified. We walked quickly through deserted, unlit streets. A full moon was shining through the bare branches of the trees and I kept looking at the moon as we walked homeward. No matter how fast and how far we walked, the moon was still overhead, keeping pace with us, following us. What an amazing discovery.

That same year, I remember walking with my mother – this time it must have been the end of December, Christmas or New Year's Eve, because my mother was wearing her long black *foka* (sealskin) coat. As we walked along a busy city street, I remember many pairs of feet, some in trousers and some in stockings and high heels. We stopped at a large store window displaying lots and lots of marvellous gifts and toys. I was mesmerized. I don't know how long I stood in front of that window; it must have taken some time to look at everything carefully. I thought I saw my mother's black fur coat to my right, but when I reached for her gloved hand, I was shocked to discover that it wasn't my mother. Mother was tall, young and blond. This person was tall also (everyone is tall to a small child), but not young, and had brown hair and wore glasses. She looked at me strangely without smiling.

Where is my mother? I am lost. What will happen to me?

All at once Mother was back. Everything was all right. We started walking again but this time I held on tight. We entered a city square full of people and stopped in front of a man wearing a white cap and an apron over his sheepskin coat. On his stomach, hanging on a wide leather strap, was a large shiny metal box. Mother said something to the man and as he opened the lid of the box, a cloud of steam came out. He took a long bun that was slit in the middle, smeared some mustard on it with a wooden spoon, put a steaming hot, pink frankfurter in it, put it on a piece of waxed paper, bent down and handed it to me. I took a bite. I can still hear the crackling sound as the skin of the hot frankfurter burst, releasing its delicious taste and unforgettable smell.

This was not a kosher hot dog. My parents were not observant, but my paternal grandmother, who lived with us, was very strict and kept a kosher kitchen, so any *treif* food had to be eaten outside the house.[1] Once, after I ate potato latkes dipped in melted bacon fat in the landlady's kitchen, Grandma Shayneh washed my mouth out with soap. Still, whenever our landlady invited me next door to eat the tasty food, I went anyway.

Even though his mother was observant, my father, Benzion, whom everyone called Bentziye, was a secular man. My father's father, Zorah Galerkin, after whom I was named, I knew only from a portrait hanging on the wall in our living room. He had a stern face with a long beard parted in the middle in the style favoured in Russia at the end of the nineteenth century. He had left Russia to marry my grandmother, whose family owned a hotel on the main street of Vilna, then part of the Russian Empire.

My grandfather died when my father was only ten years old. As to the hotel, it burned to the ground sometime during World War I and my grandmother, whose family had been well off, all of a sudden found herself a widow with three small children and very meagre means. My father put himself through high school by doing odd jobs, then apprenticed with an accountant and became what was called a *buchhalter*, a profession that combined the work of a bookkeeper and auditor. In his spare time he taught himself to play the mandolin, which he played beautifully most evenings after dinner.

～

I'm walking in the York cemetery again even though it is minus twenty-three degrees. It is a bright winter morning and the snow on

---

1   For information on the term *treif*, as well as on other foreign-language words and expressions contained in the text; historical, religious and cultural terms; major organizations; significant historical events and people; and geographical locations, please see the glossary.

the fields glistens in the sunshine. The sky in the west is a Technicolor turquoise, fading into pale blue overhead, and there are scattered white clouds like balls of cotton, some with a greyish tinge on the bottom.

I enjoy the walks in the cemetery. It is quiet, of course, and with all the trees and bushes almost like a walk in the country, but I think there is more to it. My eye is drawn to the names and dates on the monuments. If the date of death shows the person died at age ninety or older, it gives me hope for a long life. If someone died young, I feel lucky to still be alive. And seeing dates around my age makes me thankful it is not my name on that stone.

In the west the cemetery borders on a forested ravine that drops down to the western branch of the Don River. I have seen raccoons there, and a fox a couple of times, but this morning I see a large grey coyote sitting between two headstones and looking straight at me. As long as I stand still, he doesn't move. After a short while I raise my walking stick and he disappears as if he were a ghost.

At the cemetery gate I meet the young woman who often jogs with her large dog and I stop to tell her not to let the dog off his leash because of the coyote. Up close I notice how pretty she is, with large, wide-set pale blue eyes that match the colour of her ski jacket. To put her dog at ease I place the walking stick behind my back and give him my free hand to smell. At once he becomes animated and ready to play. As he licks my hand and jumps around on the leash, the mixture of his yellow and black fur makes me think of Rex.

~

Rex was my first dog. In 1939 he was five years old, same as me; my father, who loved dogs, got him as a puppy for me when I was born. He was smaller than the dog in the cemetery, but similar in colour with the same short hair. He was a smart dog, independent and serious, and didn't cause any mischief. Rex knew when my father would be riding his bike home from work and would go to meet him up the block. After dinner, when my paternal grandmother began drinking the first of many glasses of tea from the brass samovar, my father would sit with his mandolin resting on his crossed legs and begin to play as Rex raised his head, accompanying the song with a kind of tremolo howl.

We were inseparable, my dog and I, except occasionally when he would be gone for an hour or two, but he always came back. What I didn't know was that on those occasions he went to visit a bitch belonging to an officer in the Polish army. The officer didn't want his bitch to have puppies by a Jewish dog. One day, Rex didn't come back. The officer had shot him, and I learned how it feels to have your heart broken. That summer, my father brought me three different dogs from the city, but none could replace Rex.

On September 1, 1939, I was playing in the yard behind the store with our landlords' children, Georgic and Luba Dzeviatnikov, when an older boy of about ten came up and told us that Germany had attacked Poland, that France and England would be declaring war on Germany and that the Germans would soon be defeated. I heard the drone of approaching airplanes. The boy, who seemed well informed, assured us they were ours. As he was leaving he turned to me and yelled out in Polish, "Żydzi do Palestyna!" (Jews to Palestine!) It was my first real encounter with antisemitism.

The first two days of the war were the last two days of my mother's grocery business. There was a run on practically everything in the little store as people stocked up against the hard times that were sure to come. The wholesalers would no longer supply the retailers as their own supplies were also cut off, and the złoty, the Polish currency, would soon be worthless anyway. My mother tried to keep the most sought-after goods for her loyal customers. On the second day of the war, when the store was almost empty, a woman came in and asked for two kilos of sugar. Apparently she was a stranger because Mother told her that she had no more sugar left. I was standing behind the counter next to a barrel half-full of sugar and, trying to be helpful, said, "There is still sugar in the barrel." Mother, thinking quickly, said, "This is salt, not sugar." Not being in on what was happening, I assumed Mother was right, but just to make sure, I wet my finger, stuck it in the barrel and tasted. It was sweet. Seeing an opportunity to help make a sale I piped up, "It is not salt, it's sugar!" That's how I learned that sometimes it is all right to tell a lie and that being too helpful is not always the right thing to do.

That evening, Father told me a story of a man and his pet bear:

"There was a man who had a trained bear and they would go from town to town and the bear would perform for people in the town square and do all the tricks the man taught him. The bear and the man were good friends and the bear loved and respected his master. One summer afternoon while walking to the next town, they stopped for a rest and the man lay down for a nap in the shade of a tree by the side of the road. There were flies buzzing around the man's face, so he asked the bear to sit by him and shoo the flies away while he slept. The bear did as he was told and the man slept soundly. But there was one ornery fly that became very bold and sat on the man's forehead even though the bear waved his huge paw inches from the man's face. And so the bear picked up a rock and smashed the fly sitting on his master's forehead."

Poland tried to resist the Germans but their poorly equipped army stood no chance against the mighty Wehrmacht and the Poles were defeated in three short weeks. Vilna, in the eastern region of Poland, was soon occupied by the Soviet army as part of the secret deal Germany had made with the Soviet Union. In 1940, there were about 60,000 Jews in Vilna out of a total population of 200,000, the rest consisting of Poles, Lithuanians and Russians. The Soviets rounded up several thousand of the bourgeoisie, mostly Jews, and sent them to Siberia and the far eastern republics in Asia. They were the lucky ones. Most survived the war.

One of the businesses where my father kept the books, a factory called Elektrit that assembled radios, was nationalized, as were all private enterprises that employed workers, so Father was out of a job. As payment for his work, he brought home a beautiful shiny radio of polished wood and gleaming brass fittings. Late in the evening he would switch it on and search the shortwaves for music. I remember what he liked most was Roma guitar music from Hungary.

We soon moved to another part of town on Rydz-Śmigły Street. To make a living, my parents opened a small ice-cream parlour and after school I would help make the ice cream by turning the large copper cylinder that sat inside another, larger cylinder filled with ice.

My most vivid memory of that year was the New Year's Eve wedding of my uncle Pesach, the youngest of my mother's brothers, to Gita Silin, the youngest of eleven children in a family of bakers. That winter was one of the coldest in memory, with the temperature dropping below minus forty degrees. My parents and I went to the wedding in a *droschke,* a horse-drawn open sleigh, the driver up front in a long sheepskin coat and a tall fur hat and the three of us in the back, snug under a huge brown bearskin. The streets were snow covered, the stars bright and twinkling overhead in the cold clear air, the sleigh's runners gliding easily over the packed snow, the chestnut horse at a fast trot, the sound of the hoofs muffled in the snow, the bells on the horse's collar jingling merrily with each step. Sitting in between my parents I felt happy and secure and full of anticipation.

The wedding was in the home of Gita's father on Subocz Street, on the outskirts of the town. The house was a long, low building on a corner facing onto a small square. Every room was filled with uncles, aunts, cousins and other relatives, and I lost sight of my parents in the crowd. There were long tables set with platters of food and bottles. I stared at a bottle containing a liquid of a most beautiful rich amber colour. I felt a hand mussing the hair on my head and looking up I saw Grandmother Michleh smiling down at me. "So you want to drink some mead on your uncle's wedding day?" she asked, pointing at the bottle with the golden liquid. Not waiting for my answer she poured some of the honey wine into a glass for me. Its strong musky aroma and sweet taste and aftertaste remains with me to this day. That was the first – but not the last – drink I had in that house.

～

On June 22, 1941, Germany attacked the Soviet Union and bombed Vilna. We were on our way to my grandparents' house in the village of Popishok, about thirty-two kilometres from Vilna, where my mother, her seven brothers and two sisters were born. We rode in the back of a wagon pulled by a small grey horse, the peasant driver up front with his whip. The unpaved road mostly consisted of two deep ruts made by wagons in the sandy soil. We had to walk beside the wagon whenever the road went up hill.

Mother was holding my two-year-old brother, Emanuel, whom we called Monik. To pass the time, my father told me stories, all of which had a moral. Here is one I remember:

"A father and son were riding in a wagon just like this one, returning home from the market. The father bought a basket of cherries for his son to eat on the way. The boy began to eat the big, ripe fruit, but the smaller, less ripe fruit he tossed onto the sandy road behind the wagon. His father told him not to throw away any fruit, but the boy didn't listen. When the basket was empty, the boy cried for more. The father stopped the horse and told his son to pick up all the ones he had thrown away. The moral? Don't waste food."

Coming in to the village, we passed the small cemetery. The sun was low on the horizon, casting long shadows from the headstones and crosses onto the grass; the shadows of the trees reached all the way to the middle of the road. The first house past the cemetery was my grandfather's. Across the road from his house was the *kretshme*, a combination inn/tavern owned by the only other Jewish family in the village.

Popishok consisted of no more than fifty or so houses with thatched roofs, inhabited by dirt poor Byelorussian *muzhiks* (peas-ants) who subsisted on grains, vegetables and potatoes, which they cultivated on their tiny farms. Most owned a cow or two for milk and cheese, and some chickens, but they were mainly fishermen. West of the village, within a ten-minute walk, was a shallow lake, the water at the shore weedy with water lilies and cattails, and full of pike, carp and many other species of fish. The *muzhiks* fished all year round, even through the ice in winter.

My grandfather Berl Goldberg made a small living for his large family by buying surplus fish and the occasional calf and selling the meat and the fish in town. He and his wife, my grandmother Michleh (Michal), weren't wealthy, but what they did have on the eve of the great catastrophe were ten grown children, eight of them married with families of their own, all doing well in the city. The exception was their youngest daughter, Faigeh, who stayed, as was then the custom, to look after her parents as they were getting on in age.

My grandparents' house was built of square logs that turned a dark mahogany colour with age. The main room was large and L-shaped around a big brick oven with a domed opening facing the short leg of the L. There was a wood fire always burning at the back of the oven. This is where my grandmother cooked and baked bread and the challah for the Friday night candle lighting.

Across from the oven opening, under a small window, stood a heavy, long wooden table with benches on each side that sat at least twelve. In the evening, several of the peasants would come to play cards with Grandfather. There was no electricity in the village of course, and the yellow light of the kerosene lamp on the huge table was not sufficient to play cards by, so two long pieces of kindling were stuck in the cracks of the logs on each side of the window. They were lit and Grandfather gave me the important job of lighting a new one when one of the pieces was about to burn out.

The next day was a bright summer morning and the sun shone through the small window, illuminating part of the table and the bench. The rest of the room remained in semi-darkness. My parents and my little brother had gone back to Vilna the day before and left me with my grandparents. It was very quiet; no one was in the house. I lay in bed and listened to the clacking of the chickens and the low moo of Grandma's cow in the adjoining barn. I got up and went to the barn, where I saw Grandma Michal sitting on a low three-legged stool, milking the black-and-white cow. As she pulled and squeezed the long nipples of the cow's udder, the milk made a hiss as it sprayed the side of the metal pail. She poured the warm milk through a linen cloth strainer into an enameled metal can and we went back to the house. The cup of milk she gave me was warm and had a strong, sweet cow smell but it tasted good, better than the boiled milk my other grandma, Shayneh, made me drink at home. With a thick slice of black bread and butter, it made for a good breakfast.

After breakfast, Aunt Faigeh came in with a basket of eggs. She took one out, pulled a long pin from the bun of her dark blond hair and used it to make a hole in each end of the egg, breaking the yolk; she shook the egg vigorously and showed me how to eat it by sucking the contents through one of the holes. Later that morning Faigeh took me with her to the potato field, which was across the road next to the *kretshme*, to dig potatoes for dinner. The potato plants stood in long rows, each green stalk as tall as me. My aunt, who was short and stocky and went barefoot, took hold of the plant with both hands and pulled it out of the ground. Some potatoes were attached to the roots and the rest, which grew in the soil beneath the plant, she dug up using a small metal shovel turned down at a ninety-degree angle, attached to a long wooden handle. It was my job to pick up each one and put it into the burlap sack. The potatoes that grew in the fine, sandy soil of Popishok had a mealy texture and were in great demand throughout the region.

Returning from the potato field, we passed a section where rye was growing. Faigeh put down the sack of potatoes and we walked several metres into the field. The stalks of grain came up to my chest and grasshoppers were jumping in front of us. It was now noon and the sun was overhead in a cloudless blue sky; there was no breeze, no

shade and it was very hot. My aunt picked some blue flowers on slen-
der stalks that grew among the rye and she gave me a bunch to carry
back to the house. The flowers had little yellow hearts and smelled
nice.

Grandma was frying potato latkes in a large cast-iron pan. The
delicious aroma was overpowering and made me very hungry. On the
table was a plate piled high with hot latkes, next to a deep dish of sour
cream. I ate till I couldn't eat any more; to this day, latkes with sour
cream is one of my favourite foods.

The next day, after breakfast, the three children of the other Jewish
family who kept the inn across the road came to see me. The girl was
about nine, one boy was my age and the other a bit younger. They
were going down to the lake and asked if I wanted to come along.
We set off, running over the field behind our house and then along a
narrow path between the fields of rye, wheat and potatoes. We were
barefoot – all the children and women in the village went barefoot
most of the time – and I had a hard time keeping up with them because the soil on the path was very hot on my soft city soles.

After a while the cultivated fields ended and our path went
through a sloping field of tall grass. The grass would be cut in late
summer and dried to make hay for the winter. The hay fields ended at
the edge of a stand of tall pine trees with little undergrowth, carpeted
by a thick layer of pine needles. Coming into the cool and dark out of
the blazing sun, I felt very small next to the giant trunks.

The trees abruptly gave way to a stretch of grassy ground strewn
here and there with bushes and boulders, and then the waters of the
large lake shimmered in the sun. The lake stretched north and south
as far as the eye could see. We stood on the eastern shore with the
sun behind us, facing a wide, shallow bay with thick green grasses
protruding from the water. Just beyond the vegetation, we saw a boat
with two men in it. Not really a boat but a punt, a shallow, flat-bot-
tomed craft with squared-off ends. The men were fishing but had no
lines or nets in the water. The man at the stern stood and pushed the

punt along very slowly with a long pole. The man in front lay flat on his stomach, his head and shoulders protruding over the square bow, and he held a wooden spear with a barbed metal tip above his head.

We stood and watched as the men turned the punt around and came back slowly toward us. The man lying on his stomach raised the spear higher above his head; the other man pulled the pole from the water and stood stock still. The boat barely moved through the grass.

Nothing happened for a long while. Then suddenly the fisherman thrust the spear into the water and, using both hands now, drew it out with a big fat carp twisting violently on the end, its scales a golden copper hue. The other man opened the neck of a large sack and in went the struggling fish. We waited, hoping to see the fisherman catch another. It takes a lot of patience to stalk and catch a fish, as I learned later in life. We started back to the farm, stopping several times before reaching the woods, glancing back to see if the fishermen had caught another.

The next day, Friday, I awoke to see Grandpa Berl standing facing the window, praying. I tried to catch the words he was speaking. I knew Yiddish and Polish, but this was neither. The Hebrew words came very fast in a kind of sing-song. As I stood beside him, I noticed something strange – on his forehead there was a small, square, black box tied to a narrow leather strap wrapped round his head. One of his arms was bare, encircled with a black leather strap. Soon he was finished and after removing what I later found out were the *tefillin* from his head and arm, he smiled at me, patted my head and left the house without a word. I had never seen anyone pray before.

That Friday was Erev Shabbos, the day before the Sabbath. Grandpa Berl had left on an errand. There was an air of purpose and urgency in the house. Grandma Michleh was kneading dough for the challah. Aunt Faigeh was peeling potatoes for the *cholent* that would be eaten the next day, Saturday, as no one cooked on Shabbos.

The method of cooking *cholent* hasn't changed in 2,000 years, although the ingredients vary from country to country and over time. On Friday evening, a large clay pot is filled with layers of potatoes, beans, barley, meat and spices. The top of the pot is sealed with dough made of a mixture of flour, egg, water and melted chicken fat, and then covered with paper and tied with string. The pot is then put in a hot brick oven to cook slowly for twenty-four hours. The result is a delicious, hot, very aromatic meal.

Looking through the window, I saw Grandpa coming up the path with a sack over his shoulder. I ran outside to see what he had brought. He emptied the sack into a tin tub standing on a table in the shade. With a dull, wet, plop-plop, a dozen or more fish of various sizes and kinds fell in. There were perch, carp, pike and a medium-sized fish called a *shlayen,* which may have been a kind of trout. I watched, mesmerized, as some of the fish were still flopping around and thrashing their tails inside the tub. A little later Grandma came out with a knife to gut and clean the fish. The pike was so huge that its head was hanging over the edge of the tub, its mouth half-open, with rows of needle sharp, inward-pointing teeth; its black eyes stared at me and on its bony snout seemed to be a malevolent smile that said, "I dare you to touch me." I poked the top of his head. Grandma said, "Don't touch the fish, he'll bite your finger off." But the pike wasn't moving. I could see its black tongue and I had an uncontrollable urge to see what it felt like. Slowly and cautiously I put my index finger into the gaping mouth, carefully avoiding the needle teeth, and touched the tongue. It felt rough and hard as bone. At that moment its head slid off the edge of the tub and I felt the sting of the teeth on my finger. Convinced the fish was alive and intent on biting off my finger, I snatched my hand back, but the teeth only dug in deeper. I must have screamed because Grandma was at my side, carefully but firmly separating me from the pike. That was sixty years ago, but the faint marks of the teeth are still there.

I often think that the longevity in my mother's family is due to the fact that their diet consisted largely of fish. Every Friday night and Saturday there was, of course, gefilte fish, which translated from Yiddish means "stuffed fish." The way my grandmother, her mother and my mother made it before the war in Europe was like this: once the pike and carp were gutted and cleaned, the fish was cut into slices about two inches thick, making sure there was a piece of fish attached to the head. This was very important, as the head was stuffed as well and served to the head of the family or the most honoured person at the table. The flesh was removed from each slice, leaving the skin attached to the backbone. Then, the flesh from the pike, carp and other fish was chopped up and mixed together with onions and spices, the slices and the head stuffed with the mixture, and the fish reassembled and cooked.

I also remember eating fish boiled with potatoes, onions and carrots, and smaller fish fried to a brown crispness and eaten whole with my fingers, like fried chicken. In addition to fresh fish there was herring packed in salt for preserving; salted fish was an important part of the peasant diet as it was cheap and available all year round. It was eaten raw for lunch or breakfast, along with tomatoes and cucumbers and always with sliced raw onions. Herring could be sliced and baked with honey and onions, or pickled in a sauce made with vinegar, spices, the milky white sperm of the male herring and, of course, onions.

Fish, onions, garlic, potatoes, tomatoes and other freshly grown vegetables, together with dark, whole grain bread, must have contributed to a healthy diet and my family's longevity. My great-grandmother Rachel-Leah Belowitsky came to Canada before the war and lived past the age of one hundred in Brandon, Manitoba. My mother's brother Yitzchak, the only one not snared by the Nazis, fought with the Soviet army from Stalingrad to Berlin and died in Vilna in 1991 at age ninety-four and, as I write, my mother is almost ninety-two. My uncle Pesach died at seventy-nine because his lungs were damaged during the German occupation. How long the other six uncles, aunts and their families would have lived, I'll never know. All were killed in 1941, 1942 or 1943. No trace of them remains.

The war was raging somewhere, but in the small village of Popishok, life went on as before. The girl and her two brothers came again and we played hide-and-seek. They counted to one hundred and I ran through the orchard, along a grey wooden fence and into the large barn belonging to the children's family. It was a huge, dim place with several stalls but no animals, some farm implements and large wooden barrels. Against the far wall a ladder leaned up to a loft where a few bales of hay lay. The rungs were too far apart for my short legs, but I managed to scramble up and hide behind a bale, sitting against the wall clutching my knees. Soon, I heard them come in. They searched the stalls and inside the barrels and then left. It was very quiet; I heard the buzzing of bees outside, then another sound, of someone climbing the ladder. I didn't move. Then she was beside me on her knees, her hands on the floor boards, a wide grin on her face, laughter in her dark eyes. She leaned closer and kissed me on the cheek, her black hair brushing my face, and then she was gone – the sound of her bare feet on the wooden floor of the barn and out the door, the pleasant sensation of her soft lips on my cheek and the strange cucumber smell of her hair all a precious gift.

Saturday was my last day in Popishok. The next day it was back to the city and the war. I never saw my grandparents and aunt Faigeh again, nor the children I played with for those few memorable days. Before summer ended, the war came to the village in the form of an Einsatzgruppe, a Nazi squad of German, Ukrainian and Lithuanian murderers whose job it was to find and kill Jews. The two Jewish families of the village were loaded onto a truck and driven westward into the wilderness of Troki where they were shot and left for the wild animals to feed on, their bones scattered in the forest.

The Fiodorovs

At the end of June 1941, when I returned home from Popishok after spending the week there with my grandparents, Vilna was under German occupation: for the Jews the war had begun in earnest. Anti-Jewish edicts were issued daily and posted on buildings all over town. A yellow six-pointed star had to be sewn on the chest and on the back of each article of clothing worn by a Jew, young or old. Jews were forbidden to walk on the sidewalk and had to walk in the gutter on the right-hand side of the road. Jewish property was confiscated.

Lithuanians, who did all the dirty work for the Germans, began what were called *hapunes*, abductions of Jewish men. They would cordon off a street and go from house to house, searching out and taking away any Jewish men they found. Once captured, the men were taken to a prison and from there to the Ponary forest and killed. Five thousand Jewish men were thus murdered in the first month of the occupation.

One early morning, the Lithuanian militia came to search the homes on our street. We lived in an apartment that had been built in the back of a large wood-frame house belonging to a middle-aged Lithuanian couple. There were flower beds in the front yard and, in the large backyard, vegetables and tall sunflower plants grew. There was also a clean, roomy outhouse to which a large tom turkey was tied by one leg with a string. It would try to attack me each time I used the outhouse. One day, standing safely out of his reach, I pissed on him.

The landlady, who was a very decent person and had befriended my mother, came to warn us of the approaching danger. My father, a short, slim, dark man with a shock of curly black hair on his head, could never pass for an Aryan. My mother, on the other hand, was a tall, beautiful woman with long blond hair made up in two braids and pinned up on top of her head, encircling her very Slavic-looking face.

My mother never panicked or despaired; she kept her composure in the face of mortal danger, always looking for an escape, no matter how hopeless a situation seemed. She quickly led Father to the back garden where there was a pile of lumber left over from when they had built on the addition to the house, had him lie down against the wall and covered him with the wood. She took my baby brother in her arms and me by the hand and came out into the front yard just as two Lithuanian soldiers with rifles came through the gate, asking where the Jews were. The landlady, who was standing on the porch, told them there were no Jews here. One of them went inside the house to have a look; the other went to the back, looked in the outhouse, went slowly through the garden and came back. My mother sat calmly on the steps of the front porch playing with the blond baby in her lap and a seven-year-old boy in short pants with ash blond hair and grey-green eyes, his face a mirror image of his mother's, sitting next to her. The older, taller one of the soldiers excused himself for disturbing us, but someone had told them that there were Jews living here, obviously a mistake, and they left.

By the first week of September 1941, the Germans were ready to herd the Jews of Vilna into two ghettos. With typical Prussian efficiency and the willing help of the Lithuanians, they first emptied an area of several blocks in the oldest part of the city, which was by then one thousand years old, and split the area into a "large" and "small" ghetto. The district was a maze of twisting, narrow cobblestone streets where the Jews of Vilna had lived, worked and prayed in dozens of tiny synagogues for hundreds of years. Most of the people who had lived there were already resting in mass graves in the pits in the Ponary forest. The remaining Jews, numbering by then about 20,000, still the size of the population of a small town, were to be squeezed into the ghettos.

On the fine, sunny day in September that the Jews of Vilna were ordered to move to the ghettos, a Lithuanian soldier, holding his rifle in both hands, came into the front yard where our family was already packed and waiting. He told us to get moving and gave Father a push with the steel-clad butt of the rifle. This time there was nowhere to hide. The announcements posted on the walls and lampposts all over the city warned the population that anyone found hiding a Jew would be hung from the nearest lamppost along with the rest of his family. This was not an empty threat. Germans were known to keep their word.

Mother carried Monik and a valise; Father carried two large valises; and I carried a bag stuffed with some clothes slung over my shoulder. All our other possessions were given for safekeeping to our kind landlady, who was wiping away tears as we left. When we came out of our side street to the main road leading to the old town, we saw that it was filled with families carrying all sorts of baggage, all trudging in the same direction.

It was a sad and silent procession, the only sound being the shuffle of feet on the cobblestones and the heavy breathing of people burdened with heavy loads. There were no guards with dogs, just the occasional soldier standing on the sidewalk, watching. There was no place to run.

~

Walking this morning in the cemetery, I hear a most unusual sound for the middle of February: the honking of Canada geese. Any other time from late spring to the end of November, it is quite normal to see one or two flocks of these birds feeding on the grass in between the monuments and one has to step nimbly to avoid the pellets of poop scattered on the walks.

Two of the geese are flying low from the east. When I look up they come straight overhead, no higher than three metres above me, and the second bird, flying to the left and slightly behind in the leader's wake, turns his head and looks me straight in the eye. Are they wintering in Canada this year just like me or is this pair of young birds still trying to find their way south?

Returning from the walk, I meet a young mother and her toddler. The woman is pushing a stroller but the child is toddling in front and stops to gaze up at me. It is a bright, frosty morning and his round cheeks are the colour of ripe McIntosh apples. The child's mother, a tall, nice-looking woman, is speaking to him in Russian. I want to say something to them in their tongue, but when I search for the words I find they are buried somewhere in my head under a mound of Polish, Yiddish, Hebrew, English and French. And so I speak in English and, in reply to my question, she tells me the boy is one year and two months old.

~

By my eighth birthday, November 10, 1941, I spoke fluent Russian without a trace of an accent. I'd been living outside the ghetto with the Fiodorov family for several weeks. The family consisted of Mr. and Mrs. Fiodor Fiodorov, his spinster sister and their three children – a girl my age, Galia, Kolia, a boy a year older, and the eldest, Fedka, whose full name was Fiodor Fiodorovich Fiodorov. To understand how I came to spend that winter with a Russian family, I must go back to the first week of September when we arrived in the ghetto.

Upon arrival we were assigned a small space in the attic of a three-storey building. It was a true attic, not an attic apartment, the roof sloping down from above the door to the bottom of the wall opposite at a distance of no more than three metres. Over the next few days every man in the ghetto was issued a *Schein,* an identification certificate. The men useful to the war effort were issued yellow *Scheine.* All others were issued white *Scheine.*

On Yom Kippur, when most Jewish men would be found praying in the synagogue, the Germans carried out the first *Aktion* in the ghetto. They sealed off the exits to every synagogue and arrested and removed anyone who didn't have a yellow *Schein.* Again, very efficient – the Germans saved time and effort by not trudging up and down stairs searching dark closets and cramped attics for Jewish men.

My father had a white *Schein,* but he wasn't religious and so we were not in the synagogue. However, it was only a matter of time before we would be caught and taken away, so my parents decided to take a chance on the outside. My baby brother, Monik, was left with Fruma and Shmuelitzik Katz and their three children, my mother's cousins and our best friends. Shmuelitzik had been a carpenter in his youth and so had the life-saving yellow *Schein.*

Leaving the ghetto was not difficult. Every morning at daybreak, parties of workers would leave through only one gate, as all other exits were sealed. My parents joined a large group of workers and I was smuggled out hidden among them. The Jews in the ghetto were like the inmates in a Mississippi prison I once saw in a movie. The prisoners were kept in open barracks in the midst of alligator and snake-infested swamps. You could run but there was nowhere to escape to.

My parents found work in a warehouse where items of value looted from Jewish homes were stored, sorted, cleaned and sent to Germany. The manager, a decent older German, pretended he didn't know that my parents didn't return to the ghetto each night, as was required; instead, they spent the nights hiding in the warehouse.

Mother took me to the Dzeviatnikovs, the people who owned the house where we once lived and where I was born. Because people living close by knew me as a Jewish child, they couldn't keep me and so Mrs. Dzeviatnikov arranged for me to stay with her sister, Mrs. Fiodorov, which is how I came to spend the next six months with this Russian family. My story was that I was the son of Mr. Fiodorov's brother whose wife had died recently.

Life outside the ghetto was harsh. What work Mr. Fiodorov could get was not enough to support his family of six. That winter we ate three things: homemade black bread, cabbage and potatoes. These three foods were served for breakfast, lunch and dinner, the potatoes and cabbage boiled or fried with onions, or made into a soup. There was tea but no sugar, honey or any kind of sweets.

The Fiodorov house, which stood on an acre of land at the very edge of town, was small and primitive. The only entrance, through the kitchen, faced a large brick oven; straight ahead was the door to the living room and on the left, a door to the bedrooms, rooms I never saw during the time I was there. Facing the oven was a long wood table with benches on each side. On the wall over the table was a dark painting of Christ. At the entrance stood a basin filled with water and a bar of soap.

Mrs. Fiodorov was very strict. Before every meal we had to wash our hands and genuflect to the picture on the wall. We ate from metal plates using either a spoon or our hands because there weren't any forks or knives at the table. The children ate as fast as possible. The outhouse in the far corner of the yard had only one seat and no one wanted to be the last in line, waiting in the bitter cold. The first one in also had the luxury of a relatively stink-free environment.

There was no running water in the house. I don't know how the women bathed, but the men occasionally went to a public bathhouse in the city. The first time I went with them, I was scared that I would be found out to be Jewish because of my circumcised penis, but the bathhouse was full of men and boys of all ages and no one seemed to notice my difference.

These public bath visits were an absolute necessity because of the lice. The long-sleeved cotton nightshirts we slept in were worn during the day as undershirts and the little parasites made their nests and laid their eggs in the seams under the arms. This provided the children with a sporting activity. On Sunday mornings all the kids would congregate in their nightshirts in the living room – where I slept on a board laid between two chairs – and destroy as many of the pests as quickly as possible. The winner was the one who killed the most in the agreed-upon time.

The two boys didn't usually play with me but Galia, who was closer to my age, spent her after-school hours with me. She was a pretty, blond girl with dimples in her cheeks. Among the books in the living room was a medical encyclopedia, where she showed me diagrams of the male and female genitals, which was very exciting for me. We had a lot of fun with that.

The week of the Russian Orthodox Christmas, the priest and his assistant came to visit. The priest was old, with a bushy grey beard, and dressed in a long black cassock. His assistant, who was dressed the same way, was young, with a black beard. We all went into the living room, where in the far corner was an icon of the holy mother and baby Jesus. Mrs. Fiodorov had told me to do as the other children were doing. Each of us genuflected in front of the icon, then stood in a row for the priest's blessing. The old priest blessed each of us in turn by putting his hands on our heads and murmuring a blessing. I was the last and when my turn came, he didn't put his hand on my head, but instead, with his finger under my chin, tilted my face up, looked into my eyes for a long while, then asked whose child I was. I said nothing. Mrs. Fiodorov explained. He looked at me again, smiled and blessed me as well. I think he was a kind man.

My mother and father were still working during the day and hiding in the warehouse at night. Every two or three weeks I walked into town to see them. It was a long walk that took me through the outdoor market, down a long street to the Vilya River, across the Green Bridge, then up the main street another two kilometres to the warehouse.

One day – it must have been at the end of October because it was a cool day but as yet there was no snow on the ground – I crossed the bridge over the river and was walking slowly along the wide street on the right-hand sidewalk. I came to a building on the other side of the street that had two long, blood-red frightening banners hanging down. The banners reached down from the top floor to the ground-level windows and had big white circles in the middle. Inside the circles were the bold, powerful sign of the Nazis – the hated black swastika.

At the entrance stood a soldier wearing a steel helmet, a rifle at his feet. I was afraid that if I came too close, he would know I was a Jew and would drag me into that terrible place and that would be the end. To me, the German was a stern, evil person with the power of life and death, according to his whim. But the sight of that mysterious building with black swastikas on red banners and the thought of the horrible power that lay within fascinated me and I kept looking at it, still feeling relatively safe on the other side of the street.

About a block further, I saw a squad of German soldiers coming my way. They were walking in single file on the sidewalk, just walking, not marching, with rolled blankets tied to their backpacks, rifles hanging from their shoulders and bayonets dangling from belts at the waist.

A soldier, even an enemy soldier, is intriguing to a seven-year-old. I stopped and stared at them. One by one they passed, not paying any attention to me. When they were almost past me, a soldier at the rear looked at me and stopped, then motioned to me to come over. I didn't move. Again he made the sign with his fingers, the palm of the hand facing up, clearly saying, "Come, come."

So he knew I was Jewish even from across the street. As far as I can remember, the thought of running away did not occur to me. I crossed the street slowly and as I approached, the German took the rifle from his shoulder. I knew I was seconds away from being shot. But the soldier put the gun against the wall, hung his helmet from the rifle and put his backpack at his feet. I looked up at him. He was a young man with a square Nordic face and straight blond hair. He bent down, took a large cookie from his pack and handed it to me. I took it, said thank you in Polish and walked back across the street. When I looked back, the German was walking away. The cookie was big and round, sprinkled with red, green, blue and white crystals. I was sure it had been poisoned. It had to be. No German would give a treat such as this to anyone unless it was poisoned.

I smelled it. It smelled delicious. My mouth was watering. I hadn't tasted anything sweet for months. I reasoned that if I ate just one bite, it would only make me sick and I wouldn't die. I took a small bite and tasted no poison. It was so good. I waited for the poison to make me sick, but nothing happened. I walked on. The urge to have another bite was overwhelming. This time I took a big bite and waited. Still I felt no poisonous effects. That was it – I would bring the rest of the cookie to my parents. But the warehouse was too far and the cookie got eaten before I got there. I didn't die.

The Ghetto

Today is March 2, 2002. It is sunny and mild, the snow is melting and, as I walk in the cemetery, I take off my gloves and open my jacket part way. Several male cardinals are perched like bright red ornaments in the top branches of the tallest trees, singing their hearts out, wooing the females who are nowhere to be seen.

It was sixty years ago, give or take a day or two, that I returned to the ghetto on a day such as this, only there were no birds, no trees and the snow had been packed into a sheet of dirty grey ice about a foot thick by the feet of thousands of people.

Sixty years, yet pictures of those days are stored in my head as in the hard drive of a computer and all I need to do is press the right key in my brain and the snapshots will appear in living colour. Is this normal or the beginnings of Alzheimer's? My short-term memory is still good, though I occasionally have difficulty in recalling a word. For now it is not something to worry about but I have a reason to be suspicious. My mother, who will be ninety-two this November, has the disease and has lost most of her memory. Still, sometimes her sense of humour shines through the fog in her brain.

In 2000, we made a small party for her ninetieth birthday. As family and friends gathered around her in the dining room of the nursing home in Montreal, I asked her if she knew what year it was. She said no. I told her it was the year 2000. And her reply, with an amused half-smile, was, "Un men lebt nokh?" (And we are still living?)

~

Throughout the last half of 1941, every now and then the Jewish police would round up the required number of Jews demanded by the Germans, one thousand or two thousand, to be handed over for shipment to Ponary, where they would be murdered. There would be panic for a few hours and then life would just go on. How could this be? By then, every adult – and even the children my age – knew that the people taken away were being killed. I remember the adults talking about a woman who came back after being shot and left for dead in the pits of Ponary.

Herman Kruk, the librarian, described what happened at Ponary in the diary he kept. He did not survive, but the diary was found after the war in the ruins of a ghetto cellar and was originally published in Yiddish.

> *Thursday, the fourth of September, 1941*
> *The first message from Ponar*
>
> *With the help of acquaintances I was allowed to speak with some of the six that came back from Ponar. One was sixteen-year-old Peseh Shlos, who lives at Strashuna #9. She declares,*
> "On the second of September, about four in the afternoon, the Lithuanians came to our homes, ordered everyone to come with them and to take nothing with them. The only thing we could take was a package of food. From there we were taken to the Lukiškės prison until four in the morning, then told to get dressed and given to understand we were going to work. From the prison we were led on foot. The men marched in front, the women behind them. The children were loaded onto trucks. They came to the place at about ten minutes before noon.
> Hardly anyone knew that we were at Ponar and hardly anyone imagined what they would do to us. But here we saw it with

our own eyes, because no more than 200 steps from us they were shooting. The men were hit on their heads and then shot later. There were mounds of dead people. Everyone gave in without resisting. All the work was done by the Lithuanians. They were led by one German. We were driven in groups of ten people to the place of execution. In the morning there was lamenting and crying. Later it became quiet. We had got used to it and there was hardly any more lamenting."

The girl recounting the story went to the execution in the last of the tens. It was already sunset. She walked to the grave with five of her relatives. They were given an order to blindfold their eyes and were told to hold hands, ten in a row. Then they were shot. She got a bullet in the arm. The bullet came into her through her mother's body. Her mother was holding her hand and stood so as to protect her. The soldier, however, noticed that [the daughter was still alive], so he pulled off her shoes and shot her again; the bullet hit her leg. She passed out for about fifteen or twenty minutes. When she came to, she tore her hand away from her mother's dead hand and she heard people speaking. She saw a woman with a child. Four of them gathered together. Among them was someone who was not wounded at all. [She] went straight back to the city. We three, she says, went in the direction of a village. They stayed overnight. One Lithuanian gave them milk, another washed their wounds. In the morning, the Lithuanian woman brought the three of them to the city and this is how they came to be here in the hospital.[2]

~

We had returned to the ghetto because we heard it was quiet, the roundups no more. In the spring of 1942, life in the ghetto had settled into a kind of routine. Most of the able-bodied men left the ghetto each morning before sunrise, organized into work parties to do slave

---

2   Herman Kruk, *The Last Days of the Jerusalem of Lithuania: Chronicles from the Vilna Ghetto and the Camps, 1939–1944.* Ed. Benjamin Harshav; Trans. Barbara Harshav. New Haven, CT: Yale University Press, 2002.

labour for the Germans. The old and the weak were rounded up in sweeps through the ghetto by the Jewish police and handed over to the Germans for liquidation in Ponary. This is how my grandmother Shayneh was murdered together with uncle Laibeh, my father's brother, who went to his death with her of his own free will.

There were no Germans in the ghetto. It was run by the Judenrat, the Jewish council that was organized into departments like a city government and headed by a prominent Jew. The Jewish police, who kept strict order, wore a uniform and armbands marked with the word "police." One summer day, we kids found out that the Jewish police were going to hang several Jewish murderers in the unused butchers' market. Apparently this gang had lured people to a basement with the promise of sugar, flour and other kinds of food for sale. Then they killed them for a gold coin, a gold watch or some other item the person had brought to trade for the food and buried them in that same basement. When we came running into the butchers' market, they were already hanging from the metal hooks on the green tiled wall where sides of beef had hung before the war.

The ghetto had a hospital, a library, a sports centre and even a theatre. Although the Germans forbid schools for Jewish children, there was a clandestine school where I attended the third grade. I especially enjoyed the library on Strashuna Street where I spent many hours in the darkened reading room, sitting at the long table reading *Robinson Crusoe*, *Gulliver's Travels*, *Treasure Island* and others recommended to me by the librarian, Herman Kruk.

For most of 1942 and part of 1943 life in the ghetto went on. What were the chances of surviving in the ghetto? Those who had no hope, who could not accept the miserable conditions, who could not shake off the despair, perished quickly. Our family of four now lived together with thirteen other people in one large room that had been a wholesale textile business. At the entrance was a small office, where an older woman lived with her grown son. Before the war they were rich, but the husband was taken away and killed, and now all their wealth was gone as well. All day, they sat in deep despair in the tiny room and cried. They would have starved if my mother and my aunt Fruma Katz hadn't occasionally brought them food. One evening, we heard yelling and screaming coming from their room. My cousin Miriam and I managed to squeeze into the space between the legs of the adults and saw the son sitting on the floor, hitting his forehead with the sharp edge of a small ax, blood running down his face and staining his white shirt with crimson blotches. His mother stood by, helpless, tearing her hair and screaming. Someone took the ax from the boy, soon the ghetto police came and took them away, and we never saw them again.

In the spring of 1942 my father obtained the life-saving yellow paper that meant he and his family were allowed to live – for the time being. This was thanks to my mother's cousin Shmuelitzik, the carpenter, who worked in the carpentry shop at the airport with his seventeen-year-old son, Noah. My father the bookkeeper didn't know how to hold a hammer and Shmuelitzik risked his life and the life of his family by protecting him. He and his wife, Fruma, also took us in and made room for our family.

Around the walls were double bunks that slept one, two, three or four; in the middle of the room stood a table with benches. My cousin Noah slept on a board laid between two chairs. (Being a teenager, he was impossible to wake for work at four in the morning, so his father had to pull out the chair under his head to wake him up.) There was no toilet on the premises. In the corner beside the door stood a large copper pot that served as a chamber pot during the night. Everyone cooperated and there were no arguments or unpleasantness of any kind; as kids we would have sensed it if there were.

But for me, the nights were something else. The chorus of snoring in the stillness of the night was quite frightening to me, as was the constant coughing of Shmuelitzik, who was a heavy smoker and suffered from asthma, the incoherent mumbling and sighs of people having nightmares, the distinctive and melodious ping of a strong stream of urine hitting the metal of the copper pot, and especially the sound one older man made by grinding his teeth all night long. I would lie awake listening to this strange cacophony of sound.

Once we managed to obtain a certain sense of security, no matter how illusory, by having a roof over our heads, we still had to have food to survive. I don't know what the rations supplied by the Nazis were but I do know that if that's all someone had, they starved. The children didn't suffer from hunger. We were lucky because our two families, the Galerkins and our cousins, the Katzes, had three men working outside the ghetto who were able to barter for food and then smuggle it in, which was pretty tricky. The way our men did it was quite ingenious. In the shop they worked in, they constructed rough tool boxes, each with a false bottom. They put some tools in the boxes and no one ever got wise to it. At home the boxes were taken apart, the food removed from the false bottom and the wood from the boxes used as fuel for cooking and heating.

Another clever tool for smuggling in food was a large carpenter's plane. It was about 1 metre long and .15 metres wide, with an adjustable blade through the middle. It was hollowed out and the ends screwed on; every time it was used for concealing food, the screws were painted over again.

There was no variety in the food we ate. There was black bread and there was soup. We had dried yellow peas and barley. From this, our mothers made three kinds of soup – pea soup, barley soup and pea and barley soup. My favourite was pea and barley. A big treat for the kids was a little sugar sprinkled on a slice of black bread, which we had once in a while.

Most of the people in the ghetto struggled to live one day at a time, hoping somehow to live long enough to survive this terrible nightmare. But there was also an organized, underground resistance movement of young men and women who had contacts with the Polish and Lithuanian resistance outside the ghetto. They were able to smuggle in some small arms and construct crude grenades. Their intent was to foment a general uprising of the ghetto population against the Germans.

This was all supposed to be done in great secrecy, but everybody knew about it, even the school kids, as well as members of the Jewish police and the Judenrat. Most of the ghetto's inhabitants, especially those with families, were against what they saw as a suicidal action. One day, in the late summer of 1943, the underground decided to oppose the Germans when they came into the ghetto to round up some Jews for deportation. There was a brief firefight on Strashuna Street and one Jewish fighter was killed. In retaliation, the Germans dynamited one of the buildings on the street.

Early the next morning a friend and I ran over to Strashuna Street to see what had happened. The front of the dynamited building had collapsed in a pile of rubble. Only three walls of the three-storey building, with some parts of the floors of the second and third levels, were left standing, so that I could see into each apartment. I felt like a peeping Tom, looking into private rooms without permission.

There was a crowd of people standing in front of where the entrance to the building used to be and my friend and I had to squeeze through their legs to see what was happening. When we got to the front, we saw several men removing bricks and pieces of mortar from the top of the collapsed front wall. Soon we could see a pair of tiny shoes protruding from the rubble, then the white socks and pink legs of what looked like a large doll. As more bricks were removed, I could see the rest of the body dressed in a faded blue gingham pinafore over a short-sleeved white blouse. Now someone came with a board and they pulled a girl out of the rubble and put her on the board. She had no head, only a bloody piece of neck sticking out from the neat white collar of her blouse. I hesitated a long time before writing this down. It is something I haven't described to anyone for sixty years, the most upsetting image from among the other horrible images I carry with me from the war years. Now that I have "set it down" I hope the load may be a bit lighter. These difficult parts are not great for my health.

Escape from the Ghetto

Spring was trying to sneak in early; half of March was mild, the snow had melted and on some days it already felt like spring. By March 21, though, the official date for the beginning of spring, winter returned with freezing temperatures and very strong winds – the Canadian winter doesn't quit easily. But the days are longer, the rays of the sun are warm and the birds, guided by the length of the daylight hours, fill the cemetery with their song. It is eight o'clock on a Sunday morning in late March and already a Chinese family of ten has gathered in a semi-circle around a headstone shaped like a pagoda, with vertical columns of Chinese characters. Each in turn bows three times towards the grave, then the formality and solemnity is broken and a loud and lively conversation drifts to where I am standing. I resume my walk. Today it takes me past a headstone with an unusual inscription:

EUGENE BOLOTKIN
CANADIAN CITIZEN

I have no idea who Mr. Bolotkin was. The name sounds Russian, like Galerkin, my family name. The Russian people were good to me, so I hope he was a good man. How proud he must have been to be a Canadian, to have this as the epitaph on his monument.

This huge land, frozen for six months of the year, is a great country where there is freedom, equality, security and equal opportunity for all. We must be thankful, but also very vigilant, for the Jewish citizens of Germany felt the same way about their homeland before Hitler.

My father's grave is in the New Jewish Cemetery in Vilna, now in the independent state of Lithuania. On the stone it says simply, in Yiddish:

BENZION GALERKIN

BELOVED HUSBAND

AND FATHER

My father died on May 10, 1943, of typhoid fever. He was no longer a citizen of Poland or Lithuania or Russia; he was no longer a citizen of any country and he had no right to own property of any kind. As a Jew, he had no rights whatsoever. His life was worthless unless the Nazis had some use for him.

I often wonder what he thought, how he felt, lying in the ghetto hospital, knowing he was dying and leaving his young wife and his two small boys helpless and without protection, surely soon to be murdered. Did he think that somehow they would survive? A woman with two little children, the mighty German Reich intent on killing them? I don't think so. Perhaps he hoped his wife and children would have a better chance without him. An end like his is hard to contemplate.

I suspect my father lacked what I think of as the traits of a survivor. He was a gentle man. It was my mother, not he, who meted out punishment for a serious breach of discipline. He had finely shaped hands with long fingers made for strumming the strings of a mandolin, or for holding an ink pen with which he shaped beautiful letters and numbers. He was a storyteller; he liked people and everyone liked him. He was perhaps too good, too soft-hearted.

The day he died I was going down the stairs as Mother was returning from the hospital. We met on the landing. She was crying. She embraced me and told me Father had died. I was nine years old and had never really gotten to know my father. What I know of him is mostly secondhand from people who knew him and whom I met after the war. I know what he looked like from a photograph, on the back of which is a sample of his beautiful handwriting.

In July 1943 Shmuelitzik Katz, our benefactor, was taken together with the other Jews who worked with him at the airport and killed. They were no longer needed.

That summer, one of the frequent epidemics that helped reduce the ghetto population broke out. This time it was diphtheria, a sickness that strikes young children by infecting the child's throat, making it swell and, if not treated, choking off the air to the lungs. It is extremely infectious and any child who got sick was immediately moved to the hospital by the Jewish health authorities. My cousin Miriam, who was the same age as I, and with whom I played cards for hours at a time, became infected. When the medical orderly, accompanied by a policeman, came to take Miriam to the hospital, they spotted me and assumed that I was infected as well, so took me too. They kept me in the hospital ward for three days and three nights. The days weren't too bad because I could play with the kids who were recovering – at least twenty of us – but the nights were scary. The screams, the crying, the noises of the people in the other wards, terrible sounds in the night of people in pain, people dying in the same place where my father had passed away a few weeks ago – all this was very frightening to me. I never did get sick, so after three days, they sent me home. I must have inherited my immune system from my mother, not my father.

There were now persistent rumours that the ghetto would soon be liquidated. One September evening, Mother told me that she and I would be leaving the ghetto that night and that I must not tell anyone. At dusk, after the sun had set, my mother and I went out the door into the long yard, but instead of turning left toward the gate leading onto Szpitalna Street, we turned right toward the gate that led to the outside, onto Zavalna Street. The exit to Zavalna Street was now a brick wall. Before reaching the bricked-over gate we turned left into a narrow lane, at the end of which we stopped at a door on our right. Mother looked back from where we had come and when she saw no one in the lane, took me by the hand and opened the door into a dimly lit passageway. At the end of the passage she knocked on another door. We heard someone removing what must have been an iron bar securing the heavy door from the inside; a man let us in and put the bar back on the door. No one spoke. Mother reached into the pocket of her dress, took out something wrapped in a small piece of cloth and gave it to the man. He unwrapped the cloth, revealing a gold coin, and examined it carefully on both sides before putting it into his pocket. Without a word, he led us through yet another door down some steps into the basement of the building.

The basement was in darkness, the only light coming from the open door at the top of the stairs. The man whispered for us to be very quiet and to follow him. We went through an opening in the wall into another room that was in darkness except for the evening light that came through a small grated opening high up on the opposite wall, the wall leading to the outside. We stood still and waited. As my eyes got used to the darkness, I could make out another man in the corner, sitting on a crate, and a stepladder leaning against the wall under the grated opening. The opening was no more than half a metre. We waited in silence for nightfall and complete darkness. Occasionally we heard the footsteps of a passerby.

When the light in the barred window finally became a grey square against the blackness, the man on the crate got up and climbed the ladder to the window. He stood and listened for a while, then removed the grate; first Mother and then I climbed out onto the sidewalk and without looking around, started walking. The street was dark and deserted and we walked quickly. Then we turned onto another street that was wider and was lit by dim street lights. This street was also deserted but suddenly, in front of us, a door opened and a man stepped onto the sidewalk. We could see at once it was a German soldier. He was looking straight at us but Mother didn't hesitate and kept walking straight toward him. Now we could see that the man was drunk; he wore no hat and the buttons on his tunic were undone. He looked Mother up and down. Mother took me by the hand and, as we went by him, he said something – it was not an order, probably a proposition. Mother's hand tightened on mine but she said nothing, just smiled and kept on walking. A few more steps and we crossed the street and turned into a narrow, dark side street.

Through side streets, alleys and soon fields in total darkness, we kept on, without moonlight or even stars to light the way. As we were crossing a large empty space, I tripped on a railway track and fell face down, hitting the second rail with my chest. The impact knocked the air out of me. I don't know how long I lay there in pain without breathing, but I gave my mother quite a scare.

When I was finally able to breathe, we continued walking to our destination, which was where I had stayed last winter, the Fiodorov house. We arrived in the middle of the night and the house was dark. Mother knocked on the door and after a while a light went on in the kitchen. Mrs. Fiodorov, wrapped in a shawl over her nightdress, opened the door. She was a tall, dark and dour woman who suffered from migraines and had often sent me into town to the pharmacy to buy a powder to relieve them. She said she couldn't take us in because there wasn't any room, but that we could stay the night in the tool shed at the back of the yard. We spent the rest of the night huddled among the tools in the little shed, shivering from the cold and from exhaustion, despair creeping into the darkness like sewer water into a basement.

At daybreak Mrs. Fiodorov brought us some bread and said that we'd have to leave immediately. After the war we found out that the reason she wouldn't take us in was that she was hiding another Jewish family in her house.

We started walking again, but where to now? Back to the ghetto was out of the question. There was no one else on the outside we could turn to. It was a bright sunny morning and Mother didn't seem to be in a panic. There was no hesitation in her step; someone observing us would have seen us as walking with purpose to a predetermined destination. And apparently she did have something in mind.

The Germans had established two labour camps outside the ghetto for Jews with special skills. One, called Kailis, was for furriers and leather workers. The other, "Hakapeh," the pronunciation of the German letters H K P, was for mechanics and carpenters. It was to Kailis that we went first. The camp was lightly guarded and Mother knew some people who worked there, so we spent the night. However, there was no possibility of us remaining there so the next morning we were again on the outside, walking through the streets of Vilna.

Walking on the "outside" sounds nice, but for a Jew it was not like a walk in the park – it was more like a walk through a minefield. At any moment we could be denounced, arrested and shot. I am racking my brain to describe how we felt at the time. Can I compare it to a pair of mice running along the baseboards in the kitchen in broad daylight, the cats dozing on the window sill? But the mice had the hope of reaching the safety of their hole in the wall. Maybe a woman of the Tutsi tribe walking through her town with a child, hoping to pass for a Hutu during the Rwanda massacres, would understand. A feeling of helplessness and hopelessness overtook us as we walked the dangerous streets of this beautiful, ancient city.

While Mother and I were wandering all over the city looking for a place to hide, my little brother, Monik, was safely sheltered with family. My eighteen-year-old cousin Noah had learned carpentry by working with his father at the airport and had been selected for the H K P labour camp, together with his family. He declared Fruma, his mother, as his wife, Miriam, his sister, as his daughter, and my brother, Monik, as his son.

Monik was five years old that year. He was a good child, smart and well-behaved. He never cried and made no demands. His consciousness was only of the ghetto; he knew nothing of freedom or even what a cookie or an ice cream was. He was small for his age, had blond hair with a gold tint and large, serious eyes. Everyone loved him, most of all Mother. How did she feel leaving him with Fruma, also a widow by then, not knowing if she would ever see him again? My mother's strength and determination is hard to comprehend.

HKP

It's early morning at the end of April, one month past the official start of spring. We've had some warm days and the grass is green, the buds on the trees big and swollen; some have already released their fresh, tender green leaves. Two days ago it rained at night and in the morning there were thousands of worms wriggling all over the roads and walkways of the cemetery.

When I look out the window at six o'clock, the roofs of the homes, the trees and the road are covered with snow. The Canadian winter, like a boxer past his prime, is trying to make a comeback. In the cemetery the new green grass is protruding from snow that is at least three centimetres deep, the bushes and branches have snow on them, and a bunch of fresh flowers of deep purple that were placed on top of a monument are sprinkled with fresh white snow. A stiff wind from the northeast is driving frozen snow pellets that sting my skin.

I spot a red-winged blackbird with scarlet paratrooper patches on his shoulders, chattering in a loud voice, "chr – chrrrrree, chr – chrrrrree."

Spring will soon be here; it feels good to be alive.

~

We walked the streets of Vilna for what seemed like hours. It was a sunny and hot September day and we had eaten little the past two days. I was tired, thirsty and very hungry. Emerging from the side streets Mother preferred, we came out onto a main street, passed the train station and approached an imposing church. Men lifted their hats as they passed the church and the women stopped, faced the church and crossed themselves. Mother took my hand and, without changing stride or looking at the church, continued past. The church seemed to be a strange, mysterious and dangerous place, and I made a mental note to avoid walking past one in the future.

Soon we were walking along a narrow, quiet street. On our left, trees and bushes dropped down to a ravine and on our right was a high stone wall. As we passed an iron gate, I could see a garden and the stone buildings of the monastery. We were on Subocz Street, the street where almost three years ago, on New Year's Eve, we had driven in the sleigh to my uncle's wedding.

Past the monastery, coming out from a curve in the road, we could see two five-storey yellow-brick buildings with many windows facing each other, surrounded by a tall, wooden fence topped with barbed wire. Before the war, these apartment blocks were built with money donated by Jewish philanthropists from abroad to house the poorest Jews of Vilna. Now it was the slave labour camp HKP where approximately 1,200 Jews worked because they were needed by the German military. Mother was going to try and get us into this camp, but how?

We walked along the narrow, unpaved streets until we saw an older Polish woman sitting on her porch, shelling fresh green peas into a dish. We stopped; the two women looked at each other and then Mother, with me following, crossed the street and greeted the woman in Polish. Trusting her instinct, she told her we were Jews and asked her if the people from the camp ever came out into the street.

Mother's judgment was right. The woman showed no surprise and said, "Yes, every evening a gang of them come out with pails to get water." They usually passed by her house. She invited us to sit on the porch with her to wait. When Mother asked this kind lady for a drink of water, she went inside and returned with both water and a cup of milk for me with a slice of bread.

As we sat there, a Lithuanian policeman came walking down the street, looking straight at us. He was tall, dressed in a fancy uniform of mustard green and shiny black boots, a shiny black belt with many shiny gold buttons on his tunic and a shiny black peaked cap. The policeman started questioning Mother as to what we were doing there, where we had come from and where we were going. Mother said we had come from visiting her sister who lived on the other side of town and were going home to Rossa, a village a few miles away. The woman of the house greeted the man by name. After exchanging a few pleasantries with her, he went on his way, no longer suspicious.

The sun was now low in the sky, casting long shadows on the street and soon we heard the clang of tin and the sound of footsteps and saw a group of people walking in the middle of the street, carrying empty pails, speaking Yiddish.

One of the men in the group was our cousin Noah. He looked right at us, but didn't say anything. When they returned carrying the pails full of water, we were put in the midst of them and were able to pass through the gate and into the prison for slave labourers, safe for the moment.

Fruma, Noah, Miriam and my brother, Monik, lived on the fourth floor of the building to the left of the gate. The room was no more than two metres by two and a half metres with a window at the far end and a wood-burning stove. There was electricity but no running water, no plumbing of any kind. There were no elevators. Fruma and Noah made room for us by constructing a second narrow double bunk bed.

Mother and Fruma worked on sewing machines all day on the fifth floor with many other women, repairing German soldiers' uniforms that were torn, mostly by bullets and shrapnel. Noah worked in the carpentry shop. The Germans in the camp were mostly not Gestapo; they were older men from the infantry and most behaved decently to the Jewish workers. The commandant, especially, was a friendly man who tried to make life bearable for the people who helped him do his job.

The kids were free to roam the passages and stairwells. A favourite place of ours was the large attic above the fifth floor, which had lots of places to hide while playing hide-and-seek. One of the boys came up with the idea that the space on the other side of a large wooden beam on top of a metre-high wall that supported the sloping metal roof would make a good *melina*, a place in which we could hide from the Germans. The next day the boy brought a narrow handsaw and over the following days, our little gang took turns sawing through the thick beam, first one cut, then another about half a metre away. When it was done, we were able to push the loose part of the beam to the other side, crawl through and replace the sawed off piece. There was no room to stand, but we could sit or lie down. The problem of a visible, fresh cut in the beam was solved with some charcoal from a piece of burnt wood and the dirt and dust from the attic floor. This was now our favourite hiding place and we would lie there, flat on our bellies, watching the comings and goings of trucks through the narrow space between the end of the roof and the wall.

Winter came and Mother was able to sew me a pair of pants and jacket out of a discarded German army blanket, the three stripes at the bottom of the blanket decorating the lower part of the pants, so that sometimes I was able to go outside and play in the snow.

One evening, a man came to our door carrying his meagre belongings in a sack and announced that he had been told to move in with us. An argument took place outside the door. Fruma and my mother insisted there was no room – where did he think he was going to sleep in this little room? – to which he replied, looking at Mother, "I can sleep with you." No sooner had he spoken than Mother reared back and hit him a roundhouse blow to the side of his head, laying him flat on his back. The man lay there a few seconds and then scrambled to his feet, picked up his bundle and disappeared down the hall.

Sometime toward the end of winter, early one grey morning, the Gestapo came to the camp and ordered everyone to assemble in the field in the back of the buildings. We saw that a gallows had been constructed, with two ropes hanging from the cross bar. A Gestapo officer came out from the barracks followed by a Jewish man and woman, their hands tied behind them, guarded by two German soldiers. Some people knew them; they had disappeared from the camp the day before, but didn't get far before they were caught. There weren't any guard towers or guards with dogs at the camp. The work parties would usually go outside and come back; they didn't try to run away. For a Jew, it was more dangerous on the outside than on the inside. The couple was hanged there and then but the man's rope broke and there were whispers that he might be spared, but the officer took out his revolver and shot him in the back of the head.

Children's *Aktion*
and the Liquidation

Spring is a time for the renewal of life. Driving up to our cottage one afternoon on a road that winds along the shore of Elephant Lake, I came across a partridge standing square in the middle of the road. I stopped the car a few metres from the bird, who stood her ground, facing my red van.

I thought the bird was crazy, or that she had eaten some fermenting berries and was drunk. Then, from the right side of the highway, one small chick came out of the bushes and then some more, until all nine of them were at their mother's feet, and she led them into the bushes on the other side of the road.

~

It was at the end of March 1944, on a cool, bright and sunny day, the beginning of spring, the time of renewal of life, that the SS came to take the children. The survivors of the camp know it by its German name, *Die Kinderaktion*. It sounds so benevolent, like kindergarten or a children's game, but on that sunny day they came to take the children to be killed. Why? Because they were of no use to the German war effort. The children had to be fed but produced nothing.

There was little warning, but word spread like wildfire and mothers and fathers began searching for places to hide their children. Mother knew someone who had built a hiding place and so we ran there, but they had no place for us.

We could hear the commotion from downstairs – the Nazis were searching everywhere. What to do? Where to hide? We were standing in the corridor as people ran by us, with Mother holding Monik tightly in her arms, Miriam clinging to Fruma's skirt. I told Mother and Fruma about the hiding place in the attic and we ran to the stairwell and up the stairs. There were people there, some rushing up, some down.

At the next landing was a little boy. I knew him. I don't remember his name but he was about my age, but smaller. He was an artist. He made magic with a pencil and paper, producing amazing drawings of people, objects and landscapes. He mostly kept to himself, did not run with our gang and did not know about our hiding place. I asked him to come with us, but he just stood there in the corner of the landing, frozen. I had to keep moving. Once more I called to him from the top of the stairs, but he remained where he was, staring at me with his large, dark eyes.

Up in the attic some people with children were already hidden behind the beam. Mother, Miriam, Monik and I quickly crawled in and pushed the cut-out log back in place; Fruma remained outside to make sure it was even with the rest of the beam, then left. We crawled as far back as we could, all the way to where the slanting roof met the floor, and waited in silence. For a long time it was very quiet and then we heard the sound of heavy footsteps coming up the stairs, then the sound of someone in the attic, walking slowly, coming closer. Mother held my little brother tightly. No one moved. I held my breath. Would the soldier see the cut in the beam? He didn't, and soon he was gone. For a long while we lay still and listened but no one else came to the attic. Slowly and quietly, we began moving from our cramped positions. I was able to look through the narrow space between the roof and the floor. I could see the gate and the area around it, a truck covered in dark green canvas inside the gate and a man in uniform standing at the back of the truck, facing a woman with a kerchief on her head who held a young child in her arms.

The soldier took hold of the child but the woman wouldn't let go; she made as if to go in the truck with her child, but the man shoved her hard and wrenched the child from her and put the child in the back of the truck. That's what I saw; that's what I remember.

How many Jewish children did they take to be destroyed, their worth unknown? The boy on the landing might have been a great painter. But I never saw him again.

～

How many musicians were there?
How many Albert Einsteins,
one, two, three?
How about the writers,
how many Yehoshuas, Singers, Roths?

How many Saul Bellows?
Any Mailers or Richlers?

The thinkers, how many Heschels?
How many Berlins?

The contrarians, the dissenters,
the revolutionaries: Did you see
any Spinozas, Marxes, Kafkas?

And oh yes, the doctors:
Any Sigmunds or Rambams?
And can you tell us what diseases
they would have cured?

Did you come across any famous rabbis,
Any Soloveitchiks,

Schneersons, Carlebachs, Kaplans?
How many Ben Gurions did you see?

And what about the women:
Who did you meet? Any Golda Meirs,
Hanna Seneshes, Emma Goldmans,
Lazaruses, Streisands?

I'm almost done: How many Woody Allens were there?
And Spielberg, of course, how many Spielbergs?
Were there a few Chagalls?

And the musicians: Did you hear
a few Sterns or Perlmans or Dylans?

I mean, a million children is quite a number.
You must have seen something, dear God.

– *David Suissa*

⌒

Fifty years after the liquidation of the Vilna ghetto, in September 1993, my mother and I travelled back to Vilna for a gathering of the people who survived. They came from America, Australia and Israel, and most were accompanied by their children or grandchildren. The "golden" anniversary was well organized, with several gatherings and trips by bus to revisit some of the sites.

One trip was to the HKP camp. The two buildings were still standing; one was being used as an apartment, but the one where we had lived with Fruma was derelict, all its windows broken, the doors and most door frames torn out. We gathered behind the buildings, the place where people were killed when the camp was liquidated. There was a raised platform for some dignitaries and for the former chief rabbi of Israel who was to conduct the memorial service. It started to rain, first lightly, then a steady rain.

I was standing at the back of the crowd when two men approached me. One of them, the shorter one, spoke to me in Yiddish, a Vilner Yiddish. He asked if I was in the camp during the war. I said yes and asked him the same question. He told me that he and the other man, his brother, had both been here. As we talked, I found out that they lived in Israel, were both retired army officers, and that the shorter one, who did most of the talking, was head of security at Beit Hatfutsot, the Museum of the Jewish People, in Tel Aviv. We looked at each other carefully; we all seemed to be of the same age, but of course there was no chance of recognition. After all, children change when they grow up and fifty years is a long time. Then they asked where I had lived and I pointed to the derelict building. "On the fourth floor over there," I said. It turned out they had also lived in that building, on the fifth floor. Now they wanted to know how I had escaped the *Kinderaktion* and I described where I had hidden. "And how did you?" I asked.

"We also hid up in the attic behind the wood beam," said the taller brother. They had been part of our little gang who had created the hiding place – the ones who brought the handsaw for cutting the beam. My little playmates of half a century ago, when the games we had played were games of survival. The winner lived. I always wondered whether my little friend the artist, the future Chagall, lost.

~

In the three months between the *Kinderaktion* and the liquidation of the HKP camp in July 1944, the children who survived had to stay hidden. Miriam, my little brother and I spent the days in the far corner of the room, in a small space between the wall and the double bunk. We played cards, we learned how to knit to pass the time and we learned to peel potatoes in such a way that the skin we peeled was as thin as tissue paper, so as not to waste any of the potato.

In the meantime, Noah the carpenter began building a *melina*, a hiding place in the event they came looking for the children they missed the first time. The place he chose was a janitor's closet directly across the hall, with one wall adjoining a one-room apartment, the other wall the stairwell.

During the night, Noah smuggled in some building materials and over several days constructed a false wall across the small room. The closet was now half its original size with a hiding place of the same size behind it. In order to get into the *melina* he cut a hole in the wall of the adjoining apartment at floor level, next to a wood-burning stove. Concealing this hole was a piece of plywood, against which was piled the wood supply for the stove. The people in the adjoining apartment shared this *melina* with us. On at least two occasions they hid us, the children, in there when the Germans were searching the buildings.

It was a hot July day when the word spread that the SS were coming to liquidate the camp. The Soviet front was approaching, the Germans were retreating and the Jews in the camp were no longer needed.

Mother and Fruma led us along the passage to the door of an apartment. We knocked and a man let us in, went to the stove and opened the oven door, telling us to crawl in quickly. There was loud, panicky knocking on the door, as more people wanted to come in. Mother went through first, then Monik, then Miriam, then me and finally Fruma. The back of the oven was on hinges and on the other side was a large room full of people, some sitting against the walls, but most lying on the wood floor. There was no more room near the wall. We were told to lie down because there were two windows facing the other building and if we were standing, we would be visible.

Soon the room was filled to capacity. The back of the stove was put in place and the two windows were closed tight. The room was sealed and as the afternoon wore on the heat was unbearable, but our thirst was even worse. There was a small supply of water and it was rationed in minute quantities. By evening the water had run out, the heat kept rising and it became difficult to breathe as the oxygen became depleted and people began to suffer from heat stroke and lack of air.

When evening came people clamored to be let out. We wouldn't last the night in there, so we were among the first to crawl out. We went back to our room to find some water. On top of the stove was a metal coffee pot and inside was some old black coffee. We each drank some and I have never again tasted anything as sweet as that cold, black, bitter liquid.

It was now night and the building was in total darkness. There were still people running here and there in the corridor looking for a place to hide. We went across the way, back to the apartment where the children's hiding place was. It was dark. Fruma lit a match and we could see the wood piled against the wall hiding the entrance. Quickly the women removed the wood and plywood. Mother poked her head in and someone asked, "Who is it?" Inside were the people who lived in the apartment – a man, his wife and one of his two daughters; the other girl had piled the wood to hide the hole in the wall and gone to look for some other place to hide. We crawled into the *melina*, but now there was no one to pile back the wood to hide us and so the other daughter climbed out, said she would find another place to hide and piled the wood back in place.

Now there were seven of us in total darkness in that tiny space, sitting on the floor or on the narrow bench against the wall that Noah had built. We sat in silence and listened. For a long time it was very quiet, yet, we waited and listened. Time passed and we listened. We all knew what it would sound like. And then we heard them, heavy footsteps approaching along the corridor, stopping, a door slamming, the footsteps coming nearer, and now here, in the room on the other side of the wall. No one moved. I heard the sound of the steel-shod boots walking in the room, then quiet. He was still there; there was no sound of the steps receding.

I listened for the sound of wood being kicked away, but instead there was a tremendous crash. He had lifted the bed and dropped it. Again the sound of steps in the room, but now receding, and then it was quiet. We didn't dare move. We kept listening. Would he come back? We sat, listening in the darkness, while time passed. Then we heard shots, faint but unmistakable. More and more shots, a machine gun firing. The shooting went on and on and then it was quiet once more.

The air was getting bad in the small space and it was becoming hard to breathe. The older man, short of breath, was gasping. I heard the sound of matches rattling in a box and then a match being struck. The sulfur head flamed but the wood of the match didn't burn; it went out because there wasn't enough oxygen. We waited and listened. For a while, total silence, then footsteps coming closer. Would they pass and continue on? But no. Someone had come into the room and was removing the wood. It didn't sound like a German soldier … who could it be? The plywood was pushed aside and somebody crawled in. A match was struck again and this time burnt well because some air came in from outside. In the light from the match we saw the daughter who had closed us in. She was covered in mud and blood; she had been shot in the right arm, which she held against her body with her left.

She told us she had been caught and taken to the back of the buildings where a long trench had been dug. The SS pushed everyone there into the trench and then they started shooting. She was hit and fell down, and then some people fell on top of her. When the shooting stopped they covered everything with earth. She lay there covered with the bodies of the dead and the earth for a long time, and then, somehow, she was able to crawl out. She said that she thought the Germans were gone; she saw no one.

Fruma lay on the floor by the hole and gathered some of the wood as close as she could, then moved the plywood to conceal the entrance. Again we listened. The young woman was very thirsty and wanted water, but there was none. We were all very thirsty, but she was in a bad way. She must have been running a high fever, for after a while she started to hallucinate. She began to shake and talk nonsense; I thought she had gone crazy, and I was afraid.

We were still in total darkness but now I could make out the outline where the exit hole was because a weak light was seeping in and, as I watched, the outline became more pronounced – the terrible night was finally at an end. A new morning was dawning and with it some hope of escape. There was now some movement in our hole, some whispered conversation. What do we do now? The Germans may still be here, better wait some more, so again we sat and listened.

Then we heard voices in the corridor, the sound of a door opening and people in the room, but not German soldiers – these were women's voices and the sound of children and they spoke in Polish. We heard them rummaging and soon they were gone and it was quiet again.

What this meant was that the Germans were most likely gone and the people in the neighbourhood were scavenging for whatever they could carry away. So after a while, when we heard no one else, we crawled out one by one, except the couple and their wounded daughter, and we went to our room across the way. Fruma and Mother quickly made up small bundles of some of our belongings, mostly so as not to be empty-handed and look suspicious. Fruma also took down from the wall a cloth bag tied with a drawstring where we kept bread that we dried out in the oven so it wouldn't go mouldy. Mother took Monik by the hand and we made our way down the steps and out into the bright summer sunlight.

Outside there were more people and children carrying bundles and we followed them towards the gate. I saw a dead woman lying just inside the gate. She was an old woman with grey hair, lying on her stomach with both arms flat beside her head, wearing a dark dress with white polka dots, heavy beige stockings and black low-heeled shoes. Her right leg was stretched out, her left one bent at the knee as if she was trying to crawl to the outside. There was no guard at the gate and people were coming and going. No one was paying attention to the body in the dust, as if she were a dead dog.

We continued walking away from the camp and although I had no idea where we were going or what would happen, it felt good to leave that place of death behind us. As we walked, an open car approached, moving fast; in it were German officers and soldiers and they passed us in a cloud of dust. So the Germans were still here, and we were still in danger of being captured and killed.

End of a Nightmare

The Canadian winter just won't quit. It is now the middle of May and I am walking down a snow-covered dirt road back to my cabin by the lake. I turn and look at my red van, which is parked at the top of the hill facing a tree lying across the road; the tree fell from the weight of the wet snow. The road back to the lake is narrow and twisting, with no room to turn the van around and too dangerous to reverse, so I'm walking back to the cottage to get a saw and an ax.

As I walk I'm watching for signs of bear tracks in the snow. When I came up to the cottage six days ago, I found the metal screen to the porch door pushed in and the steel frame bent out of shape. Down by the dock the bear had torn apart the Styrofoam cooler box that still had the smell of the fish from last fall.

It starts snowing again, heavy wet flakes. There is total quiet in the woods except for the dull sound of wet snow falling off tree branches and as I walk down the road, a large partridge explodes into the air with a great rush of beating wings.

There are only eight other cottages on our lake and there is no one in them as the weather so far has been miserable. Also, my phone is out of order and I didn't bring my cell phone. If I don't move that tree, I'll be stuck here for at least another five days. I tap my right pants pocket to make sure that my nitroglycerin spray is there. I may have to break into one of the cottages to use their phone, but what if the main line to the lake is down?

I return to the van with my handsaw and ax. After clearing away the branches, there is just enough room for the van to pass under the tree, which is leaning against another tree across the road. Another bit of good luck.

~

It was a hot, sunny day in the middle of July 1944. Two women carrying bundles and leading three small children didn't raise any suspicion. We were walking to the *kominy*, which means chimneys in Polish, a neighbourhood about five kilometres away, on the other side of town where Fruma and her family had a big house and business. It was too dangerous to walk on the main road because too many people knew her there, so we had to take a longer, roundabout way.

She led us off the road into some woods not far from her house, then up a hill where among the tall pines we found a trench dug most likely by some soldiers as some kind of defensive position. There was no one in the woods, so Fruma told us to climb into the trench and wait for her. She herself would go down to see some of her neighbours whom she could trust.

It was pleasant on the hill among the pines and even though it was a hot afternoon, the air was dry and breezy and I soon fell asleep in the shade of the trench. I woke up when I heard Fruma's voice. She had returned with a few boiled potatoes tied up in a kerchief and a jar of milk. Fruma was a few years older than my mother, of average height with light brown hair tied in a bun and a fine, light complexion with rosy cheeks. She was very energetic, always busy doing something, and stood for no nonsense from anybody. She and Mother were like sisters. She told Mother that there wasn't anywhere to hide out here but she had a plan. We would walk to Charnobur, a village about fifteen kilometres away where Fruma was born and grew up, and where she had a good friend who might be able to help.

By now it was evening, too late to start out and the women decided that we should spend the night in the woods and start out early in the morning. As the sun set and night fell we settled down in the trench and I was soon fast asleep. Suddenly, I was awoken by a blinding white light that shone right through my eyelids. I saw above us something that looked like a bright star with rays radiating from it, descending slowly. I heard the drone of airplanes, the shrieking whistle of a falling bomb and, finally, an explosion that shook the earth. Then more earthshaking explosions preceded by the nerve-wracking shriek of the bomb and flares in the sky, turning night into a strange, bluish-white daylight. Even at the bottom of the trench we were completely exposed, everyone's face a contrast of white planes and black shadows.

Mother was holding my little brother in her arms, Miriam was clinging to Fruma and I was sitting with my back against the wall of the trench, looking up at the sky. I wasn't afraid. These were Soviet planes, piloted by Russians; they were bombing the Germans and I was totally confident we wouldn't be harmed by these liberators in the sky. I remember feeling grateful that someone was finally coming to rescue us. Fruma said there was a munitions factory not far from where we were and that the Soviets were trying to bomb it. Eventually the last of the flares burnt out, the bombs fell further and further away and soon it was dark and quiet again and I fell asleep once more.

The next time I awoke it was with a feeling of dread. I heard a man's voice speaking in German and opened my eyes to see a German soldier standing above us on the edge of the trench, holding a rifle. We all looked up at him and didn't move. Assuming that we didn't understand what he was saying, he spoke in a broken Polish, "Go home, bomb finished." Then he disappeared.

I looked out over the lip of the trench. Although the sky was a pale blue, the sun was not yet up and a low-lying mist in the trees was making everything look grey. There was no sign of the soldier who had taken us for Poles.

We left the trench and descended slowly from the hill. At the bottom, the woods ended at a dirt road. With Fruma leading, we crossed the road and went down into a field of tall grass sprinkled with purple, yellow and blue flowers. The air was fresh and cool and we were walking down a narrow path running straight east toward the sun. The long grass, wet with dew, bent toward the middle of the path and brushed my bare legs with a pleasant coolness. The scent of grass and flowers was strong and I felt good, almost happy, and all at once I got the urge to run.

I ran past Fruma and Miriam. I ran down the path through the wet grass, scaring some birds that flew away, twittering in panic, and as I ran faster I felt so light I imagined I could fly away just like those birds. When I reached a small rise in the field I stopped and looked back – the others were far away, so I lay down in the grass, picked a handful of the long stems and began to chew, extracting a sweetish milky liquid from the thick stems while waiting for the others to catch up.

Finally, we came out to a major road, the one that would take us to the village of Charnobur, but after walking for some distance, we encountered too many people, horse-drawn wagons and a truck full of German soldiers. Fruma led us back into the woods and we continued walking along a path that ran alongside the road. But even here we met people going the other way and it felt as though our luck was about to run out.

It must have been close to noon, for the air in the forest was hot, even in the shade. We weren't far from the village when a man walking toward us blocked the path. He was short and wiry, in his forties, wearing a dark suit and hat and his small face was tinted grey, with the stubble of hair of several days. In his clenched fists he carried a sturdy staff, with which he now blocked the way.

"I know who you are," he said. "You are Jews."

He had recognized Fruma. The women pleaded with him to let us go, but he wouldn't budge. Mother took my father's gold watch from her wrist and gave it to him. As she handed him the watch, his gaze fell on the two wedding rings on her fingers. She removed them quickly and he took them also. Then Fruma removed her wedding ring and gave it to him as well. All the while, Mother and Fruma were begging him to let us go.

Through the trees we could see a convoy of German soldiers going toward Vilna, most likely retreating from the Russian front. The man, holding his staff like a weapon, ordered us to stay there and walked quickly to the road, stopping one of the trucks in the convoy. He spoke to the soldier sitting next to the driver, all the while pointing at us.

I thought for sure that this was the end and was getting ready to run into the forest, but then the German, whose arm was hanging out the open window of the truck, gave a dismissive wave with his hand and the truck took off, leaving the man standing in a cloud of dust. Not waiting another moment, we took off at a fast pace toward Charnobur, glancing back to see if the man would come after us. Fortunately, we never saw him again.

Fruma's friend lived on an isolated farm that bordered one side of the forest near the village. There was a small house where the family lived and a large barn that stood some distance away on the fields between the house and the woods. It was in that barn, up in the loft where the hay and straw were kept, that Fruma's friend let us hide.

We stayed up there several days, maybe a week, without incident. Fruma's friend would come to the barn, usually at dawn, and bring some bread, potatoes, water and sometimes milk. There was nothing to do but look out at the fields and the woods through the cracks in the boards of the wall, but I saw no one, not even an animal. I don't know if we were there for three, four or ten days, as each day was exactly the same as the one before.

One morning as I lay on the hay, half-awake, waiting for the sound of the farmer's wife bringing food, I heard something from the direction of the woods. I quickly put my eye to a small hole in the edge of the board and looked out. Coming from the forest were several soldiers holding long rifles or machine guns, walking slowly toward the barn. A shiver went up my spine, my scalp tingled as the blood rushed to my head. Then I felt a surge of relief as if a threatening cloud had dissipated, letting the sun shine again. In the sharp, clear light of the early morning I had no doubt at all – these men were our liberators, soldiers of the Red Army.

I told Mother and Fruma and then scrambled down the ladder and ran out the barn door, Mother and the others following behind me. The soldiers stopped and waited for us to approach. The one in front, who must have been an officer, wore a round peaked hat with the red star on it and was holding a submachine gun with a round magazine attached, like the ones you see in the gangster films of the thirties. He was dressed the same as the others, in faded khaki shirts and pants tucked into dusty leather boots. The soldiers behind him wore long army caps without the peaks, the red star on the front, and were armed with rifles. As a group they did not look intimidating; they were smaller than the German soldiers we had seen the week before.

I was the first to speak. I said in Russian, "We are Jews." Mother, who was now beside me, also spoke in Russian, telling them we were hiding in the barn from the Germans. The reaction from the officer was not what I expected. As far as I knew, most, if not all, the Jews of Vilna had been killed. I didn't imagine that anyone else from our camp had survived, so I expected that we would be taken to a safe place and treated as celebrities. Instead, the officer looked around before saying anything, as if he expected to see something beyond the barn and the house. He told us that there were still Germans around and that we had better stay hidden another day or two. The Russians continued past the barn and past the house toward the village. Reluctantly, we went back to the barn and stayed there overnight.

The House on Subocz Street

It is now the middle of July on a Sunday morning in Toronto. The rising sun illuminates the monuments, bushes and trees in a clear, strong contrast of light and dark. There is no one on the cemetery grounds at this hour. I turn off from the main road onto a narrower path that crosses a small creek, the banks lined by trees and bushes.

On the green lawn between the bushes and the monuments, I spot a large brownish rabbit grazing on the grass. Moving slowly and quietly along the edge of the bushes, I'm able to get within a few metres of the animal before he hops away and hides in between two small shrubs in the shade of the monument of the Chung family grave. He sits there and keeps one big, unblinking black eye on me. I move nearer but in a roundabout way. The sun has now cleared the monument and is shining through the rabbit's ears, which are raised in alarm. Something has chomped off about a third of his left ear, a dog or a fox or maybe another rabbit in a fight over a female. We stare at each other, eye to eye, for a long time, and when I make a move he hops away, showing his white tail, shaped like a ball of cotton.

By now, I feel the heat of the sun. After a while I come to a favourite spot for a brief rest. It is a stone monument standing in the shade of a spreading Manitoba maple. The grave contains the ashes of:

BORYS STERNBERGER

1922–1992

On the headstone are engraved pine trees, mountains and two stars. Many times I wonder, was he a German, or an Austrian from the Alps? Born in 1922 he could have been a soldier fighting the Russians or in the SS killing Jews. Or maybe he was a submariner or even a Canadian of German ancestry. I have this difficulty with men of that age, men from Germany, Austria, the Ukraine, Hungary, Croatia, the Baltic states of Lithuania, Latvia and Estonia, and even Finland, all the ones who fought against the Allies in World War II. There is no way of telling if they have the blood of innocent men, women and children on their hands.

~

Fifty-eight years ago almost to the day, also on a very hot and sunny day, we came out of hiding in the barn in Charnobur and started on the road back to Vilna. The soldiers of the Red Army and the partisans were chasing the Germans back to Germany, capturing some, but mostly killing them by the hundreds.

It wasn't long before we came upon the bodies of German soldiers lying on both sides of the road. They must have been dead for at least a couple of days, for the bodies bore no resemblance to the smartly dressed, proud and arrogant Germans we saw during the occupation. The corpses were bloated grotesquely; most had been stripped of their uniforms and boots by the local peasants and their rotting skin was an ugly blackish-purple colour. Black flies were buzzing about and the stench was unbearable.

We left the road in order to avoid the sickening smell and continued through the woods that bordered the road on both sides. This time there was no traffic on the road and no people on the paths. What most likely had happened to the Germans was that the Soviets ambushed the retreating troops and cut them down in a crossfire from the forest, soaking the soil with the blood of the invaders. The rotting Germans on the road were no longer a threat to me and, at last, it felt good to be free of fear.

We arrived at Fruma's house on the outskirts of Vilna late in the afternoon and moved into half of it; the other half remained for the people who had lived there and taken care of it during the occupation.

Although the threat of death no longer hung over our heads and we had a place to stay, we now faced starvation: there was no food anywhere. The only way to get food from those who had some was to barter but we had nothing to barter with – the last things of value, my father's gold watch and the wedding rings – had been taken by the man who tried to turn us over to the Germans. During the first few days, we subsisted on the few potatoes and some black bread Fruma's neighbours were kind enough to part with. Most of it went to the children; the women ate almost nothing.

～

At the outbreak of the war in 1941 I had eight uncles and two aunts, most married with children, as well as three grandparents. My grandparents perished and only two of my uncles survived the Holocaust. The others disappeared without a trace, together with their families.

One uncle who survived was the youngest of my mother's brothers, Pesach Goldberg, and his wife, Gita. It was their wedding on New Year's Eve, 1940, that I remembered so well, where my grandmother Michleh let me have my first sip of honey wine. Pesach was only twenty when they got married. He was the shortest of the seven brothers, stocky and very strong, with reddish-blond hair and freckles on his face and hands. He was lively and resourceful, always able to find a way out of a difficult situation, the traits needed for survival.

In 1942, the Nazis established a slave labour camp in the forest not far from the village where he was born. There, the men cut turf for burning, which was back-breaking work. There were about two hundred Jews in that camp, among them another of my uncles, Tzalel, the eldest. Tzalel was twenty years older than Pesach and I remember him vaguely as being very tall and likable. The work was hard, but both my uncles were strong and used to hard work, and the Germans treated the workers decently.

Every morning, the men were counted. One morning, several men were missing, having escaped during the night. The Nazis, great believers in collective punishment as a disciplinary tool, made up a list of ten men to be shot. The men of the camp assembled in a quadrangle and as the commandant read out the names on the list, each man had to step forward and join the chosen. The last name on the list was Goldberg. Before Pesach could move, my uncle Tzalel stepped forward and joined the other nine.

Pesach and Gita survived in the HKP camp and escaped through a tunnel before it was liquidated. After liberation, they reclaimed a part of her father's property on which the big, old house where they got married stood. As I said, my uncle was very resourceful and I don't know how, but he got a hold of a diamond-tipped, glass-cutting tool. Since there was fierce fighting in Vilna before the Germans gave up the city, many buildings were demolished or damaged, and half the windows in Vilna were broken. Pesach went around and fixed or replaced the broken panes, for which he was paid in food or any items of value his customers were willing to part with.

A little of the food was given to Mother, but it was not enough to feed five people, so it was decided that I would go to live with Gita and Pesach. That way, whatever food there was could be divided in four portions instead of five. And so it was that the next year would be the most happy and carefree of my childhood.

Gita's father's house stood on the corner of the market square on Subocz Street. Part of the property behind it was a large field where potatoes, onions and other vegetables grew. At a distance of about sixty metres from the house stood the outhouse. Beyond the property there were more grassy fields, actually pastures, that sloped gently towards the Vileyka River, a smaller river that ran through the town and emptied into the much larger Vilya. On the other bank of the river was a very steep sandy rise topped by the dark green of a pine forest. This was Bellemont. There was a legend that when Napoleon passed through on his way to Moscow and saw it, he exclaimed: "Quelle belle mont!"

It was in this river that I learned to swim – mostly against my will. Within a few days of my arrival, I was accepted into the neighbourhood gang of Polish boys and girls my age. We would go down to the river, raid the orchard for berries and fruit on the way, and then most of us would go swimming naked in the river. When I refused to go in, saying I couldn't swim, I was stripped of my shorts by several boys and girls, and then four of them took hold of my hands and feet and threw me into the deep pool. I had to swim or sink. I thrashed about for a while and found that if I moved my arms and legs, I didn't sink. This is how I learned to do the dog paddle.

That summer, I also learned how to fish with a line made of braided hair taken from a horse's tail. For a hook we used a safety pin and the rod was a long, thin branch. Some days we would cross the river and climb Bellemont Mountain, then go deep into the forest to collect mushrooms, look for blueberries and raspberries on the edge of the clearings and try to smoke dry rolled-up leaves as if they were cigarettes.

Life in the city and in Gita's father's house slowly returned to normal. The house, built of logs, was spacious but old and without any amenities. There was no running water; the water was brought in pails from a well across the street. The entrance to the house was from the back, the side facing the fields, the river and the heights of Bellemont above it. To the left of the entrance was a long room, part kitchen but more a bakery, a large stone baker's oven at the far end. Beyond and to the right were more large and small rooms, with windows facing the market square.

By now, more Jews who had survived, mostly young people who fought as partisans in the forests around Vilna, returned to the city. Many would stop for a day or two at the house before moving on, but two brothers, Benjamin and Yankl, and their sister, stayed. These two young men were also bakers. Delicious little buns and bagels were baked during the night and in the early morning Gita and the bakers' sister took them to be sold at the market in the city.

Where did they get the flour, salt and sugar for the baking? Well, Uncle Pesach, ever-resourceful, got a job that put him in charge of supplies for the prison now located in the old monastery on Subocz Street. He became good friends with the Russian commandant by supplying him with vodka, cigarettes and other luxuries. That is how business was done in the Soviet Union in those days. Those who took chances on the black market and were clever lived well; those who were caught spent years in Siberia.

There was plenty of food now to make up for the hungry years – eggs that my uncle fried with bacon every morning, preceded by a glass of *samogonka*, a very potent homemade vodka, which he taught me to drink the Russian way, in one shot. There were fresh vegetables and ripe tomatoes from the monastery gardens, grown by the prisoners, as well as milk, sour milk, salted butter, herring with onions and potatoes and of course, freshly baked bread, buns and bagels.

That summer, a Russian tank division stopped in the forest across the river and took over the bakery to bake bread for the soldiers. The bakers were two old Ukrainian soldiers. They baked at night and sat around in the afternoon smoking thick cigarettes that they rolled by hand in newspaper. One of them was especially nice to me. He would invite me to sit beside him, tell me stories of the war and let me take a puff from his cigarette. He also let me shoot his gun from World War I, which was longer than me and very heavy. The first time I fired it I put it against my shoulder and squeezed the trigger. The powerful recoil hit my shoulder with such force that it knocked me flat on my back. The old soldier had a good laugh and then showed me how to brace myself with my right leg behind me, how to reload and how to fix and remove the long bayonet of the ancient rifle.

The real shooting would take place on an evening when the radio announced that another major city had been taken from the Germans, who were retreating all along the front. On these occasions, all the men in the house, including the Ukrainian bakers and usually some visitors who were there for a drink of vodka, came out to the field behind the house and emptied a full magazine of their firearms into the air. The shooting started all over the city and continued for several minutes. These were shots of joy and triumph, and it was all very satisfying for me.

One morning, there was a treasure hunt in the potato field out back. Gita's father had been a wealthy man and before the large family was dispersed after the Germans swept in in 1941, he told her that he had buried gold coins and jewellery in the potato field. So after the potatoes were harvested, all of us, armed with spades and shovels, began digging for gold, row by row. I was the lucky one. My spade hit something shiny and golden among the clumps of black earth. I called out to my uncle and we all gathered around and dug up a large tin can of a golden colour. The can was sealed like a can of sardines. Everyone dropped their shovels and with great anticipation, trooped into the kitchen where my uncle proceeded to open the can with a can opener. Inside was well-preserved ham.

What had happened to the treasure and how the can with ham got buried in the potato field was a mystery, but the dig was not a total waste, for the meat was tasty and cold, as if taken from an ice box, and with tomatoes, onions, black bread and a shot of vodka, made a good lunch.

Life was good to me that first summer, the days full of sunshine, and my predominant feeling was of being free and carefree after being liberated from the dark nightmare that had consumed one-third of my life. But there was one exception.

Some weeks after my arrival in Gita's house, I went to visit my mother for the first time. She was still living with my little brother, Fruma and Miriam in Fruma's house. Mother asked me to go back to the HKP camp, to the hiding place on the fourth floor, and look for a bar of soap in which she had hidden her last gold coin. She was sure that this was where she lost it.

I don't know how Mother and the others obtained food to keep from starving. Whatever little food sent to them by my aunt and uncle was not enough to feed the four of them, so finding that bar of soap with the gold coin was essential.

It so happened that the camp buildings were also on Subocz Street, the same street where I now lived with Gita and Pesach, but nearer to the city. The day that I was returning after visiting Mother, I had to pass the former camp and as I came closer the familiar stench of rotting flesh hit my nose. On the ground were the partially decomposed corpses of the Jews who were killed and buried in a shallow common grave when the Germans liquidated the camp.

My aunt and uncle were there with others to identify and rebury their relatives. Gita identified the bodies of one of her brothers and his family. That day, I did not go in search of the gold coin.

The next morning, I walked with a heavy heart down Subocz Street toward the camp. When I stood outside the fence at the opening where the gate used to be, I gazed up at the forbidding yellow-brick buildings with the black window openings, now devoid of windows, staring back at me like blind men with empty eye sockets. I felt an awful dread come over me and a great reluctance to go through the gate and back into that place.

I forced myself to leave the safety of the street and go inside. As I walked into the dim corridor of the silent, empty building and up the grey stone steps littered with debris, feelings of evil and danger returned.

I arrived at last in the room that led to the hiding place. I stood in front of the hole that was the only entrance to this dark place that held so many bad memories. Most vivid and terrifying was the memory of the young woman, her left arm shattered by a German bullet, bleeding and covered with the dirt that was soaked with the blood of the people who fell on top of her as they were being slaughtered.

I knelt in front of the hole in the wall and poked my head and shoulders through. Inside was total darkness. I could see nothing.

How could I look for the bar of soap without even a match to light the place? I crawled all the way in and once my eyes got used to the dark, was able to make out the faint features of the narrow hiding place with the bench against the wall. I had a strong feeling of claustrophobia and a desire to run away but I summoned all my willpower to fulfill Mother's request. I knelt on the dirty floor, using the palms of my hands to feel along the walls and under the bench. I searched, but found nothing.

The rest of the summer of 1944 continued to be enjoyable. More survivors hidden by gentile friends came out of hiding and many of the Vilna Jews who survived the slaughter by fleeing to the Soviet Union began returning.

In the fall of that year I was enrolled in the fourth grade of the Jewish school. It wasn't much of a school; it was located in an apartment on the second floor of a row of apartment buildings on the shore of the Vilya River. As far as I can remember, it consisted of no more than two classrooms. It was far from where I lived and it took a good hour for me to get to school. What I remember most of that school year is a day in the spring of 1945 when class was interrupted in midmorning and the thirty or forty students of the school assembled on the sidewalk in front of the building together with the teachers. We were told that the American president, Mr. Roosevelt, a great friend of the Jewish people, had died. We were sent home for the day.

Walking back from school one day – it must have been in October 1944 because the weather was still warm – I again passed the camp buildings on Subocz Street. I noticed that there was a new gate at the entrance and in front of it stood a Russian soldier wearing shiny black boots, with a submachine gun across his chest. I went around to the side where there was a low hill outside the fence and was able to see the field behind the building. What I saw gladdened my heart – behind the fence topped with barbed wire where the Germans had kept us imprisoned, the yard was now full of German prisoners. I stood there a long time, trying to get used to this reversal of fortune.

There were the Germans and here I was, not thirty metres from the fence, yet I was safe and felt no fear. The prisoners paid no attention to me; as a matter of fact, most were absorbed in watching a game of volleyball being played in the centre of the field. Finally, the players' and spectators' guttural shouts in German made me uncomfortable and I went home.

Some weeks later, I heard that a group of the prisoners who were working in the forest cutting wood returned to the camp with a bag of mushrooms they harvested and cooked a nice mushroom soup, only some of the mushrooms were poisonous and several Germans died; many more got very sick. I realize now that the reversal of fortunes was not quite as equal as I thought then. The difference was that the imprisoned Jews were sentenced to die and most were killed. On the other hand, the German prisoners were waiting to be set free and eventually were; most went home to their families.

Later that year I remember sitting at the large table in the main room of Gita's house doing my homework, writing in a notebook with a pen. I dipped the pen into a small glass bottle of ink that stood open on the table. As I lifted the pen to dip it into the bottle to get more ink onto the nib, the little bottle, of its own free will, jumped up and turned over, spilling the ink all over my homework and the table. I stood there looking at the mess, wondering how to explain to Gita the big black stain on her table. Then, I heard excited voices outside. I looked out the window and saw several people standing in the middle of the otherwise empty market square looking up, some pointing in the direction of the city. Once outside, I looked up and saw a thick column of black smoke, the top shaped like a mushroom, rising high into the sky over the distant town.

Since there were no telephones, no one knew what had happened, but within a short time the news reached our neighbourhood that an ammunition train had been blown up in the railway yards. Fruma's house was about a kilometre past the railway yards but much closer than we were, so it was decided that I should go see if they were all right. I left at daybreak the next morning. As I neared the train station, I saw debris on the street and broken window panes in the buildings. As I came nearer still the ground was littered with large pieces of splintered wood, twisted metal and chunks of artillery shells and pieces of bombs, the bright yellow explosive material still sticking to the round metal skin of the bombs. On the street running parallel to the railway tracks there was a dead horse lying in the road. I don't remember seeing any people; it was as if I was the only living being in that vast devastation.

On my walks to visit Mother I always stopped in front of a low one-storey building that faced the tracks and would watch the workers inside taking red-hot molten glass from the roaring oven and then blow into it, their cheeks bulging, all the while twirling the long tubes, creating hand bottles and jars of various shapes and sizes. That building was now gone, everything blown away by the blast, even the massive brick oven.

Turning past where the glass factory used to be, I took the street going up a steep hill that would lead me to Fruma's house about half a kilometre away. I rushed past many houses badly damaged by the explosion, but once I got to the other side of the hill the houses seemed mostly all right, though the road was still littered with debris.

Fruma's house was undamaged but in the front yard, not more than six metres from the porch, lay the iron wheel of a railway car that had been carried there by the force of the blast. Everyone in the house was all right. One more piece of good luck.

That winter, I learned how to skate on the frozen river below Gita's house. Someone gave me one old rusty skate and I cleaned it, polished it and sharpened it until it looked almost new. Still, it was only one skate, which I wore on my right leg attached to my boot with a leather strap; a special fitting on the heel of the skate fitted into a hole made in the heel of the boot. To this day I skate much better on my right leg than I do on my left.

There were many boys and girls skating up and down the ice,

and one day I saw a boy around my age skating the other way. His long pants and jacket looked very familiar. I turned around and followed him for a while, until I recognized the unusual outfit. The suit was of a dark grey woollen material and the pants had three light grey stripes below the knee. This was the garment my mother had stitched together for me while working in the camp, using pieces of the German army blankets that she was repairing for them. Those pants were one of a kind.

The Accident

In the fall of 1994 when my mother was eighty-four years old, I got a call from my half-brother, Joe, that she was critically ill: she was in the emergency ward in Montreal's Jewish General Hospital. Leaving the business with Franciska, my baker, I started on the six-hour drive from Toronto to Montreal together with Lillian, my wife.

We learned that Mother had had an attack of pancreatitis, a disease in which the canal from the pancreas becomes blocked. In a person of such advanced age, as my mother was, it is usually fatal. But that night the doctors managed to clear the blockage, so that by morning she was out of danger and we returned to Toronto.

However, when we arrived at the bakery in the afternoon, there was a message to call the hospital. The doctor came to the phone and told me that Mother had suffered a massive heart attack, was in intensive care and that she might not last the night. We got back in the car and again started for Montreal. The trip was most difficult because it soon grew dark and a heavy rain began to fall, becoming more intense as we drove east. The mood in the car was as dark and gloomy as the weather, with the thought of Mother dying hanging like a black cloud over our heads.

We arrived at the hospital late in the evening. The intensive care unit was dark and quiet except for the beeping of the life-support monitors. Mother was lying partially upright in a bed, tubes hanging from her arms, an oxygen mask under her nose. She was unconscious and the heart monitor was beeping weakly and irregularly. The nurse rolled two chairs over to the bed and we sat there a long time, waiting. Her eyes were closed, her breathing shallow and laboured, and she seemed to be in distress. If she was sleeping, the dreams were nightmares. At last her eyes opened and Lillian, who was like a daughter to her, spoke to her gently, but she did not recognize her and began to thrash about as if to leave the bed. She looked at me and said clearly in Yiddish, "Men darf layfn in vald." (We must run to the forest.) She was back in the war, running from the Germans. She was in danger of disconnecting some tubes, so I put my hand on her shoulder to make her lie down on the bed and said to her in Yiddish, "Gay shlofn, mameh" (Go to sleep, ma) to which she answered angrily, "Go to sleep yourself."

My mother was not yet ready to go to sleep; she was fighting death as she fought the Germans, using every fibre of her being and every ounce of her strength to stay alive, the same will to live that brought her and her two sons through the nightmare of the ghetto and the camp.

It was past midnight. I left the phone number to my mother's apartment, where we would be staying, and asked the nurse to call at once if "something" happened. The nurse promised to do so, but her manner did not encourage optimism. We went to bed expecting the phone to ring any minute with the sad news that Mother had died.

But the phone did not ring and so, by seven in the morning, we were back at the hospital. We went straight to intensive care but Mother was no longer there. I was convinced that she had died in the night and they hadn't called us. The night nurse was gone and, after asking at the nurses' station, we were told that she had been moved to a room. After wandering about, we located the right room number and, walking in, were astonished to see Mother sitting up in bed, eating breakfast. Although one-third of her heart muscle was dead, she eventually recovered and went back to her upper duplex where she lived on her own and climbed the two flights of stairs several times a day.

~

May 1, 1945, was the date of the big May Day parade in Vilna. Our class walked in that parade; there were red banners and bands playing the "Internationale" and the hymn of the Soviet Socialist Republic. It was a hot and sunny day and there was more standing around than walking. When we saw ice cream vendors on the sidewalk, a few of us sneaked away from the parade and ate ice cream that was sold from an icebox, all one flavour, vanilla. Each square piece was wrapped in wax paper and the ice cream was soft and ran down our hands and faces. Then we went down to the Vilya to wash up and ended up swimming naked in the ice-cold river.

On May 8 the war ended. Hitler was dead and there was a happy, euphoric mood in the city. That night there was a long and loud fusillade celebrating the end of the war and the defeat of the Nazis. Two days later, I went to the shul on Zavalna Street, the only synagogue not destroyed in the war, to say Kaddish for my father on the second anniversary of his death.

On May 13, five days after the end of the war, a man I didn't know came to Gita's house. He had come from the *kominy* area where Mother and Monik lived with Fruma. He came straight over to where I was standing. As I looked up into his serious face, he told me that Monik was dead, killed on the road in front of Fruma's house by a speeding truck.

I felt as if I had been dealt a terrible blow to the chest. All at once the dread and darkness of the war years returned and I wanted to hide again. I ran to the corner of the room and crouched behind a bed, invisible, hidden again. They understood and left me alone and I stayed there a long time. When the shock wore off somewhat, I came out from my hiding place and set off with the man on the long walk to Fruma's house.

In the far corner of the front room stood the bed Mother usually slept in. She was lying there now, crying and moaning, clutching to her breast the pale, cold, lifeless body of my little brother.

New Beginnings

My cottage stands on six piers made of concrete blocks on a steep hill overlooking the lake. There is a wide wooden deck that runs the length of the house that faces the lake, with a long staircase descending to a steep path that winds among the trees and leads to the dock.

There are only nine cottages, all on the north shore, and many days I am the only human being on the small lake, but if I am patient I can observe the non-human inhabitants. This spring, the pair of loons has again hatched two fluffy brown chicks that swim close to their parents or ride on the back of one of them. The pair of otters has also produced a pair of pups and are very aggressive, hissing and barking at me if I approach them. There is the great blue heron that stands motionless in the shallows near the shore then strikes lightning fast with his long beak and comes up with a minnow or a frog or tadpole every time. Occasionally, the osprey swoops down and ascends with a thrashing trout in his talons.

A beaver swims by the opposite shore, dragging in his mouth a long white branch of the birch tree like a small tugboat pulling an ocean liner. As night falls, the bats soar swiftly on silent wings just above the surface of the lake, picking off mosquitoes on the fly, and the hoot of the owl seems to come from all directions. Then, as the moon rises in the starlit sky, the howling of the wolves in Algonquin Park mixes with the piercing cry of the loons, accompanied by the chorus of a thousand frogs croaking and peeping, sounds as pleasant to listen to as a symphony by Mozart.

Late in the evening the chief of the local raccoons, a big fearless fellow, comes up the steps to the deck to check out what's been cooking on the barbecue, then walks over to the window and stares at me with unblinking eyes; if he could speak he would most likely ask when there will be more fish guts to eat.

This spring a robin built her nest in the crook between a branch and the stem of a young pine tree about fifteen metres from the deck. The top of the tree is at eye level to a person standing on the deck so that the nest, being near the top, is visible, though hidden from view from the ground. In the nest, which is no bigger than the cupped hands of a child, are three small eggs the colour of the sky. This particular bird is exceptionally beautiful, her colours more vivid than the robins in the backyards of city homes. When not sitting in the nest she is busy flitting about, chasing away a blue jay whose territory overlaps hers.

One sunny morning when the rays of the sun hit the nest, the eggs were gone; in their place, three little beaks protruded over the edge of the nest. Then there was a change in the weather, a strong east wind that brought heavy grey clouds and a driving rain. As I came up the path from the lake, carrying a speckled trout for dinner, there was a rumble of thunder in the distance. The wind was now a gale and the tops of the trees were swaying violently. During the night it stopped raining but the wind didn't let up. Gusts of wind rattled the windows and blew the smoke from the logs burning in the old Franklin stove back into the cabin. Lying in bed that night listening to the wind howling, an old English lullaby came to mind.

> Rock-a-bye baby, on the tree top
> When the wind blows, the cradle will rock
> When the bough breaks, the cradle will fall
> And down will come baby, cradle and all.

Sure enough, in the morning the robin's nest and the chicks were gone. I found the empty nest in the bushes by the path but there was no sign of the young chicks. But when I came back two weeks later, there was a new nest in the pine tree with two pale blue eggs in it.

～

In the summer of 1945, after the death of my brother, my mother came to live with me at my uncle's house. With the end of the war a period of rebuilding and renewal began. Cities that had been flattened to rubble and lay in ruins – Stalingrad, Warsaw, Berlin, Tokyo – were rebuilt. The survivors of this terrible war also began to rebuild their shattered lives.

My mother, who was only thirty-four that year, had three men who wanted to marry her. One was Lazar the baker, short, dark and very lively, constantly talking and joking. When he was alone with her, he tried to hug and kiss her. Another was a major in the Russian army, the commandant of the prison where my uncle Pesach, whom he called Petia, short for Piotr, supplied food for the prisoners. Their relationship at work was mutually beneficial and profitable. Often he would come for lunch on a Sunday, accompanied by one or two other officers and the table was set with a variety of herrings, cold cuts, fresh vegetables and foods prepared by my aunt and my mother. There were bottles of vodka within easy reach of everyone, fifteen or twenty guests, men and women alike, eating, drinking, having lively conversation. The major sat at the head of the table and everyone deferred to him. When he spoke in his deep baritone, everyone listened.

I remember in particular one discussion concerning Israel, which was then called Palestine. Many of the people around the table were making plans to settle there, in what they hoped would be a Jewish state. The major, having downed a few glasses of vodka by then, said, "There can never be a Jewish state." Why? "Because the Jews have survived for two thousand years among non-Jews by outsmarting them and fooling them. Whom are they going to fool in a Jewish state?"

The third man was Maisheh Rotszyld, who came from a small town near Popishok, the village where Mother was born, and who had courted her when she was sixteen and seventeen. He survived the concentration camps where his wife and their three children were killed.

One evening in the late fall of 1945, Mother was waiting for me in front of the house. It was getting dark and the street was deserted. She put her hands on my shoulders and told me that she needed to get married, that we needed a man to take care of us, but she would leave it to me to decide who should be my stepfather.

The choice was between Lazar the baker and Maisheh Rotszyld. The Russian major, whom I would have preferred, was not a choice. I didn't like how Lazar was always cornering Mother and putting his hands on her, so I chose Maisheh, whom I didn't know at all. That month, I was twelve years old. On January 1, 1946, on the fifth anniversary of the wedding of Gita and Pesach in the same house and the same room, my mother and Maisheh were married.

In the spring of 1946, Fruma and Miriam, together with Noah and Ester, Miriam's older sister who also survived, left for Palestine with Mania, Noah's new bride, and Maisheh Kraichik, Ester's new husband. Ester was seventeen years old and both she and Mania were pregnant. Miriam, Ester and Noah had seven children between them and many grandchildren. They all live in Israel.

Fruma left her house to my uncle Yitzhak. He and his wife, Luba, fled Vilna before the Germans occupied the city and were in Minsk when the war broke out. He was drafted into the Red Army and fought the Germans from Stalingrad to Berlin. He returned to Vilna in the spring of 1946 and remained there until his death at age ninety-four. His son Grisha and his two children live in Saint Petersburg (formerly Leningrad); the younger son, Yossi, lives in Israel with his two children.

Gita and Pesach immigrated to Canada in 1959 with their daughter, Chana. She and her husband and three of their four children live in Calgary; their eldest lives in the United States.

My mother, stepfather and I left Vilna in July 1946, planning to go to Palestine, but due to the pogroms in the south of Poland we were scared to travel through it and had to remain in Poland until 1949, when we finally went to Israel. There, my mother, at age forty, gave birth once more to a boy, my half-brother, Joe. He lives in Montreal with his two sons.

I married Lillian Blumenfeld in 1956 in Montreal, where we raised our two daughters – Sandy, who has three children, and Barbara, who has two – and we all now live in Toronto.

And so the saplings that remained standing after the great conflagration passed over the Jews of Europe grew into strong trees with many branches.

My mother, who has by now lost most of her long- and short-term memory, will be ninety-two on November 15, but her good nature and warmth toward everyone still shines through the fog in her head. She is liked by all the staff in the nursing home and by most of the residents, the ones who are still coherent. All day long, she carries around with her a doll, which she holds in her arms like a baby.

If you know Yiddish and listen carefully when she speaks to the doll, saying "Shainer, kleiner yingeleh" (beautiful little boy), it is to the little boy whom she lost almost sixty years ago that she speaks. This is one memory that she will take with her to the grave. The doll was a present for Mother's birthday from Dayna, my eight-year-old granddaughter.

Epilogue

In the summer of 2005 I received a phone call from my cousin Yaffa, who lives with her husband and three children in Jerusalem. She is the daughter of Noah Katz, who in his late teens, after his father was killed by the Germans in 1943, took over as head of the family and helped his mother, his two sisters, my mother, brother and me to survive.

Yaffa asked if I was coming to Israel next month to attend the ceremony at Yad Vashem, the Holocaust museum and memorial, for the induction of Major Karl Plagge, the commandant of HKP, into the ranks of the Righteous Among the Nations, a designation given to gentiles who saved Jews at great risk to themselves. This was a surprise but then, as more information became available to me about this German officer, I began to realize that our survival in the labour camp was due to a large extent to this commandant, a decent German with a conscience and courage.

I was not completely surprised. As a child of nine or ten I met, or rather was near, when he happened to walk by, an older man with greying hair at the temples and a small moustache, walking with a slight limp, dressed in the grey uniform, black boots and long coat of a German officer. I remember that I felt no fear when he glanced at me as he passed by. Young children, like dogs, can instinctively recognize danger emanating from someone. Quite likely I must have heard from the adults that he was a decent and friendly man who tried to make life bearable for the people who helped him do his job. I later found out that before the camp's liquidation, he managed to warn the Jews that the SS were coming, allowing hundreds to go into hiding.

After the ceremony in Jerusalem, which was attended by several of the survivors from HKP and some of Plagge's relatives (he died in Germany in 1957), I spoke to Yaffa again and she gave me the phone number of a man from Toronto she met at the ceremony. His name is Lazar Greisdorf and he also survived the camp as a young child with his parents and brother.

When we were liberated by the Soviets in 1944, I had imagined that the only survivors from the camp were our family and a few others. Now, after all these years, it turns out that about a quarter of the Jews, about 250 out of approximately 1,000 imprisoned in the camp, survived. Considering that only about 2,000 of the 60,000 Vilna Jews remained alive by the time the Nazis were chased out, the number of Jews who survived the camp seems out of proportion. And so it turns out that the commandant, Major Plagge, was instrumental in saving my life as well as the others.

The story of his efforts to save as many of the Jews imprisoned in HKP as possible is told in the book *The Search for Major Plagge* by Michael Good, whose mother was one of the survivors of the camp.

Glossary

Aktion (German; pl. *Aktionen*) The brutal roundup of Jews for forced labour, forcible resettlement into ghettos, mass murder by shooting or deportation to death camps.

antisemitism Prejudice, discrimination, persecution and/or hatred against Jewish people, institutions, culture and symbols.

black market An illegal and often informal economic system. With the inherent shortages and bureaucratic complexities and constraints of the Soviet economic system, many people risked participation in an underground black market to get ordinary goods and services, or informally bartered or traded within it. As a matter of everyday survival, most citizens knew how to steer through a complicated and often corrupt bureaucracy.

British Mandate Palestine The area of the Middle East under British rule from 1923 to 1948, as established by the League of Nations after World War I. During that time, the United Kingdom severely restricted Jewish immigration. The Mandate area encompassed present-day Israel, Jordan, the West Bank and the Gaza Strip.

cholent (Yiddish) A traditional Jewish slow-cooked pot stew usually eaten as the main course at the festive Shabbat lunch on Saturdays after the synagogue service and on other Jewish holidays.

Einsatzgruppe (German; pl. Einsatzgruppen) A mobile death squad responsible for the rounding up and murder of Jews in mass

shooting operations. They were a key component in the implementation of the Nazis' so-called Final Solution in eastern Europe.

Gestapo (German; abbreviation of Geheime Staatspolizei, the Secret
State Police of Nazi Germany) The Gestapo were the brutal force
that dealt with the perceived enemies of the Nazi regime and were
responsible for rounding up European Jews for deportation to
the death camps. They operated with very few legal constraints
and were also responsible for issuing exit visas to the residents
of German-occupied areas. A number of Gestapo members also
joined the Einsatzgruppen, the mobile killing squads responsible
for the roundup and murder of Jews in eastern Poland and the
USSR through mass shooting operations.

ghetto A confined residential area for Jews. The term originated
in Venice, Italy in 1516 with a law requiring all Jews to live on
a segregated, gated island known as Ghetto Nuovo. Throughout
the Middle Ages in Europe, Jews were often forcibly confined to
gated Jewish neighbourhoods. During the Holocaust, the Nazis
forced Jews to live in crowded and unsanitary conditions in run-
down districts of cities and towns. Most ghettos in Poland were
enclosed by brick walls or wooden fences with barbed wire. *See
also* Vilna ghetto.

HKP (German; abbreviation of Heereskraftfahrpark, vehicle repair
park) A group of army vehicle repair workshops in Vilna run by
the Wehrmacht under the supervision of the SS. One HKP unit
was a forced labour camp for Jews established by Wehrmacht Major Karl Plagge outside the Vilna ghetto in September 1943 – after
he learned about the ghetto's impending liquidation. The camp
employed between 1,200 and 1,500 Jews, many of whom were actually unskilled labourers whom Plagge was trying to protect. *See
also* Plagge, Karl.

Internationale A well-known and widely sung left-wing anthem.
Adopted by the socialist movement in the late nineteenth century,

it was the de facto national anthem of the Soviet Union until 1944 and is still sung by left-wing groups to this day.

Jewish ghetto police (in German, Ordnungsdienst; literally, Order Service) The Jewish ghetto police force established by the Jewish Councils on the orders of the Germans. The force, armed with clubs, was created to carry out various tasks in the ghettos, such as traffic control and guarding the ghetto gates. Eventually, some policemen were ordered to participate in rounding up Jews for forced labour and transportation to the death camps. There has been much debate and controversy surrounding the role of both the Jewish Councils and the Jewish police. Even though the Jewish police exercised considerable power within the ghetto, to the Germans these policemen were still Jews and subject to the same fate as other Jews. *See also* Judenrat.

Judenrat (German; pl. *Judenräte*) Jewish Council. A group of Jewish leaders appointed by the Germans to administer and provide services to the local Jewish population under occupation and carry out German orders. The *Judenräte*, which appeared to be self-governing entities but were actually under complete German control, faced difficult and complex moral decisions under brutal conditions and remain a contentious subject. The chairmen had to decide whether to comply or refuse to comply with German demands. Some were killed by the Nazis for refusing; others committed suicide. Jewish officials who advocated compliance thought that cooperation might save at least some Jews. Some denounced resistance efforts because they believed that armed resistance would bring death to the entire community.

Kaddish (Aramaic; holy) Also known as the Mourner's Prayer, Kaddish is said as part of mourning rituals in Jewish prayer services, as well as at funerals and memorials.

Kailis (Lithuanian; fur) A fur factory outside the Vilna ghetto where approximately one thousand Jews worked as forced labourers, relatively protected until July 1944; most were murdered by the

Nazis in the Ponary forest before the Soviet Red Army liberated Vilna. *See also* Ponary.

Kinderaktion The SS-coordinated roundup and murder of children in the ghettos and concentration camps. Children were singled out in part because they required food but were too young to be effective workers. The children in the HKP labour camp were murdered in a planned action on March 27, 1944. Approximately 250 children were killed that day and the rest, fewer than two dozen, remained in hiding until the camp was liquidated three months later. Karl Plagge, the camp commander, was on leave during this time. *See also* HKP; Plagge, Karl.

kosher (Hebrew) Fit to eat according to Jewish dietary laws. Observant Jews follow a system of rules known as *kashruth* that regulates what can be eaten, how food is prepared and how meat and poultry are slaughtered. Food is kosher when it has been deemed fit for consumption according to this system of rules. There are several foods that are forbidden, most notably pork products and shellfish.

Kruk, Herman (1897–1944) A Polish Jew from Warsaw who fled to Vilna at the beginning of the war. Kruk, a librarian, painstakingly chronicled life in the Vilna ghetto and the labour camps in Estonia in diaries, which he buried. Hundreds of pages were recovered after the war and published in Yiddish in 1961 and in an expanded edition in English in 2002, titled *The Last Days of the Jerusalem of Lithuania.*

May Day Also known as International Workers' Day, May Day is celebrated on May 1 in many countries around the world in recognition of the achievements of workers and the international labour movement. It was first celebrated in Russia on May 1, 1917. In countries other than Canada and the United States – where Labour Day is considered the official holiday for workers – May Day is marked by huge street rallies led by workers, trade unions, anarchists and various communist and socialist parties.

Plagge, Karl (1897–1957) A Wehrmacht officer who tried to help Jews in Vilna during World War II. Although a Nazi party member, Plagge didn't ascribe to Nazi ideology and his position afforded him some ability to protect the Jews under his care. Post-war documents and survivor testimony attest to his character and efforts, which included establishing the HKP forced labour camp outside the Vilna ghetto before its liquidation and convincing the SS that the working men needed to have their wives and children with them for motivation. Plagge also hired unskilled labourers to do vehicle repair and obtained work permits for shoemakers, hairdressers, gardeners and tailors. Unlike most other SS officers, he demanded that the camp guards treat the workers with decency and respect. Before the HKP camp's dissolution, Plagge made a speech in the presence of SS officers in which he carefully warned the camp population of its impending liquidation. This information allowed hundreds of Jews to heed his warning and hide. Of the 2,000 Vilna Holocaust survivors, 250 were from the HKP camp. Karl Plagge was awarded the honour of Righteous Among the Nations in 2005. *See also* Righteous Among the Nations.

Ponary (Polish; in Yiddish, Ponar) A forest seven kilometres from Vilna that was the site of mass killings of Jewish and Polish civilians between July 1941 and August 1944. During this period, Nazi officers and Lithuanian collaborators murdered approximately 70,000 Jews and 20,000 Poles. A memorial and museum were erected at the site after the war.

Righteous Among the Nations A title bestowed by Yad Vashem, the Holocaust Martyrs' and Heroes' Remembrance Authority in Jerusalem, to honour non-Jews who risked their lives to help save Jews during the Holocaust. A commission was established in 1963 to award the title. If a person fits certain criteria and the story is carefully corroborated, the honouree is awarded with a medal and certificate and commemorated on the Wall of Honour at the Garden of the Righteous in Jerusalem.

Sabbath (in Hebrew, Shabbat; in Yiddish, Shabbes, Shabbos) The weekly day of rest beginning Friday at sunset and ending Saturday at sundown, ushered in by the lighting of candles on Friday night and the recitation of blessings over wine and challah (egg bread); a day of celebration as well as prayer, it is customary to eat three festive meals, attend synagogue services and refrain from doing any work or travelling.

tefillin (Hebrew) Phylacteries. A pair of black leather boxes containing scrolls of parchment inscribed with Bible verses and worn by Jews on the arm and forehead at prescribed times of prayer as a symbol of the covenantal relationship with God.

treif (Yiddish) Food that is not allowed under Jewish dietary laws. *See also* kosher.

Vilna ghetto A September 1941 Nazi decree established two ghettos in Vilna, one for skilled workers, who were given work permits, and the other for those unable to work. One month later, Einsatzgruppen squads murdered ghetto inhabitants who were sick, elderly or weak, shooting more than 20,000 into pits that became mass graves in the Ponary forest. The mass killings continued until the end of the year. In January 1942, a resistance movement, the United Partisan Organization (in Yiddish, Fareinikte Partisaner Organizatzie, or FPO), was formed in the ghetto but was generally unsupported by the majority of inhabitants; hundreds of its members eventually fled to nearby forests and joined partisan movements. Between the spring of 1942 and 1943, the Vilna ghetto population remained relatively intact; roundups began once again in March 1943. By the end of September, the ghetto had been liquidated, with thousands either murdered in Ponary or sent either to the Sobibor death camp or to labour camps in Estonia and Latvia. The Soviet Red Army liberated Vilna in July 1944. *See also* Ponary.

Wehrmacht (German) The German army during the Third Reich.

Yad Vashem The Holocaust Martyrs' and Heroes' Remembrance Authority established in 1953 to commemorate, educate the public about, research and document the Holocaust.

Yiddish A language derived from Middle High German with elements of Hebrew, Aramaic, Romance and Slavic languages, and written in Hebrew characters. Spoken by Jews in east-central Europe for roughly a thousand years from the tenth century to the mid-twentieth century, it was still the most common language among European Jews until the outbreak of World War II. There are similarities between Yiddish and contemporary German.

Yom Kippur (Hebrew; literally, day of atonement) A solemn day of fasting and repentance that comes eight days after Rosh Hashanah, the Jewish New Year, and marks the end of the high holidays.

Photographs

1

2

1 Steve Rotschild's paternal grandmother, Shayneh Galerkin (back row, far right),
   with friends in pre-war Vilna. Circa 1920.
2 Maternal grandparents, Berl and Michleh Goldberg. Vilna, circa 1920.

1 Steve Rotschild's parents, Esther and Benzion Galerkin. Vilna, circa 1930.
2 Steve Rotschild, age three.
3 Emanuel (Monik) Galerkin, Steve's brother, approximately age one.

Steve and his mother with the Dzeviatnikov family. Standing in back are Mr. and Mrs. Dzeviatnikov; in front, left to right, are Steve; Luba Dzeviatnikov; Steve's mother, Esther Galerkin; and Georgic Dzeviatnikov. Vilna, 1938.

1 Steve and his mother after liberation. Vilna, 1946.
2 Steve and his mother visiting Monik's gravestone in the Vilna cemetery, 1993.

Steve Rotschild (left) with cousins Ester (centre) and Miriam (right) after the war. Vilna, 1945.

1 The HKP labour camp buildings, as seen in 1993.

2 Courtyard of Szpitalna #9 in the former Vilna ghetto, where Steve Rotschild lived after staying with the Fiodorov family. Photo taken by Steve Rotschild, 1993.

די 2 בנינים זיינען אויפגעשטעלט געווארן דורך באראן הירש
אין יאר 1898 אלס ... אכטשאפט פאר ... ישע יידן אין ווילנע.
אין יאר 1941 האבן די נאצי־מערדער ארויסגעטריבן די איינוואוינער
... אין געטאָ. די אינגעלעך זין פאנאר. האט די זיינען דערמאָרדעט
געווארן. דורך די נאָפיס דים דיערע ארבעטער סיסטעמלעך פאר דעם
די 2 היינער זיינען פארוואנדלט געווארן אין א צוואנגס ארביים
לאגער וועלכער האט געהייסן H.K.P. דא האבן געארבעט פעם בורך
2500 מענטשן. פאראן אן קאמער. דער באמטער פיל אין דערמארדעט
געווארן אין פאנאר.
בערך 500 מענטשן. פאראן אן קינדער האבן די נאָפיס דערמארדעט
דא. ... אן זיינען באגראבן אין גרויבער ארום די היינער.

THESE TWO BUILDINGS WERE ESTABLISHED BY BARON HIRCH
IN 1898 AS A DORMITARY FOR THE NEEDY JEWS OF
VILNA TILL 1941.

IN 1941 THESE TENNANTS WERE EVACUATED BY THE GERMAN
NATZIS TO THE GETO AND WERE SLAUTHERED IN PONAR.

THE NATZIS TURNED THE TWO BUILDINGS INTO A WORKING
CAMP NAMED H.K.P. FOR 2500 PEOPLE WHO WORKED THERE
AND WERE MURDERED IN PONAR.

ABOUT 400 PEOPLE WERE MURDERED IN THIS VERY PLACE
BY THE GERMAN NATZIS AND THEIR LOCAL ASSISTANTS
AND WERE BURRIED HERE IN THEIR BACKYARDS IN HOLES
IN THE GROUND.

Memorial plaque at the site of the HKP labour camp. 1993.

Index

The Azrieli Foundation

The Azrieli Foundation was established in 1989 to realize and extend the philanthropic vision of David J. Azrieli, C.M., C.Q., M.Arch. The Foundation's mission is to support a wide spectrum of initiatives in education and research. The Azrieli Foundation is an active supporter of programs in the fields of Education, the education of architects, scientific and medical research, and the arts. The Azrieli Foundation's many initiatives include: the Holocaust Survivor Memoirs Program, which collects, preserves, publishes and distributes the written memoirs of survivors in Canada; the Azrieli Institute for Educational Empowerment, an innovative program successfully working to keep at-risk youth in school; the Azrieli Fellows Program, which promotes academic excellence and leadership on the graduate level at Israeli universities; the Azrieli Music Project, which celebrates and fosters the creation of high-quality new Jewish orchestral music; and the Azrieli Neurodevelopmental Research Program, which supports advanced research on neurodevelopmental disorders, particularly Fragile X and Autism Spectrum Disorders.